BEATING THE BIG ONE

Ask anyone who has been in the North A
an unfriendly place. Storms are an every
common. Many have died simply as a re
where life expectancy is measured in minutes. but the
fascinates, and has done for at least a thousand years, since the earliest
documented crossings by the Vikings Eric the Red and his son Leif.

Most journeys by open boat have been the result of necessity — indeed,
Eric had been banished from Iceland, and Ernest Shackleton's and William
Bligh's epic journeys in more recent times were equally forced upon them,
albeit in different circumstances. Alan Priddy decided to do it in the best
traditions of British explorers: to prove that it could be done.

To say that he succeeded is inadequate. He and his crew have created
untold goodwill on both sides of the Atlantic, raised considerable money
for charity, and inspired a whole new generation of "RIBsters", those
people who drive small, powered, rigid-hulled, inflatable-collared craft,
appropriately referred to as the four-wheel drives of the sea.

To organise a voyage of these epic proportions takes a person of immense
character and persistence. Priddy not only prepared the ground himself,
but the boat too, fitting it out with everything he thought he and his crew
would need to survive their journey. The fact that they did survive is
credit to his planning, workmanship and responsibility. He had help, of
course, from his crew, his family and friends, and from many suppliers,
sponsors and supporters, but it is still a monumental enterprise.

The bare bones of the story make interesting enough reading, but the
experiences and pictures brought back by this heroic crew are fascinating.
The agonies, the fear, the exhilaration and the wonder are all there, as well
as intricate details of all aspects of the historic voyage, from several
preparatory adventures to detailed planning and eventual execution. It is
a story to inspire, excite and intrigue anyone who loves the sea. It will
probably never be repeated, let alone surpassed, and Priddy and his brave
crew of Jan Falkowski, Steve Lloyd and Vic Palmer can dine out for years
to come on their place in maritime history.

If anyone with a small boat can read this book and ever again be fully
satisfied with pootling around their local coastal waters, then they must
have very little imagination indeed. You have been warned!

TONY HOLKHAM

Born in a Nissen hut in 1948 in Mitcham (then in Surrey), Tony Holkham was always a writer at heart, but on leaving Churcher's College in Petersfield, he worked first in a bank for four years, then in industry for a further 21 years. He finally achieved his goal of becoming a full-time writer in 1992, when he started working on his first book *Label Writing and Planning — A Guide to Good Customer Communication*, an entertaining, irreverent but immensely practical book for producers of consumer goods (published in hardback by Chapman and Hall, 1995).

Tony's second book, like *Beating the Big One*, was also about the sea. *Challenge* is an inspiring, amusing and touching account of the 1996 Multiple Sclerosis Society-backed Multiple Challenge, a round-Britain sailing relay crewed by MS sufferers. Tony took part as a helper on one leg of the voyage, and has pledged the profits of the book (and an accompanying video for which he wrote the script) to the MS Society.

As well as books, some short stories, poetry and drama, Tony regularly writes articles and letters on a wide range of topics based on his interests in the environment, society and consumer affairs. His third book, a light-hearted but helpful consumer advice manual, *Don't Take It Lying Down* was published in 1997. He is currently working on two other books and looking for interesting projects for the future.

Tony is a keen gardener, avid reader, dabbles in several musical instruments and has fitted out and is learning to sail his own dinghy (but only when it's sunny). He is also interested in astronomy and space research, and often wonders why visiting spacecraft never break down...

BEATING

THE BIG ONE

The story of the first high-latitude crossing of the
Atlantic by open boat in 1,000 years

by

Tony Holkham

Safe T net

THE BIG ONE
© 1997 Alan Priddy & Tony Holkham

Published by Safe T net
22 Willowbed Drive, Chichester, PO19 2JB England
Telephone 01243-537333   Fax 01243-787303
E-mail 101716.1612@compuserve.com

Font: Palatino 10 point. Typeset in Quark XPress™.

Printed by Holbrooks Printers Limited
Norway Road, Hilsea, Portsmouth PO3 5HX
Telephone 01705-661485   Fax 01705-671119

ISBN 0 9520305 5 1

Also by Tony Holkham and/or available from Safe T net. (Full list available on request)

Challenge: The story of Multiple Challenge 1996, A Round-Britain Sailing Relay
With a Foreword by Tracy Edwards, MBE
Paperback, illustr., ISBN 0 9520305 3 5, £9.99 +£1 p&p
Accompanying video (CTC Publicity), 30 mins, £7.99 +£1 p&p. Both £15.99 +£1 p&p
60 sufferers of multiple sclerosis proved, by sailing a yacht in relays round Britain's coast in all weathers, that contracting this awful disease need not signal the end of an active life. Factual and entertaining, it is an inspiration to sufferers of this and other incapacitating illnesses, and also a useful companion to anyone sailing Britain's coastal waters.

Don't Take It Lying Down
Paperback, 1997, 250 pages ISBN 0 9520305 2 7, £9.99 + £1 p&p
An amusing and immensely practical book detailing the author's experiences with creditors, suppliers and other matters during a three year period of illness. Despite enormous financial pressures from every direction, Tony managed to keep his head above water, principally by writing the right letter at the right time. Full of useful tips, angles, tricks and even some questionable (but always lawful) tactics for today's beleaguered consumer.

Label Writing & Planning — A Guide to Good Customer Communication
Hardback, Chapman & Hall 1995, 240 pages, ISBN 0 7514 0361 X, £27.50 + £2 p&p
A dig in the ribs of consumers and a kick up the backside of industry, this book tells in a lighthearted way not only what is wrong with product labelling, but how to put it right, in detail. Selling worldwide, it is the only labelling bible, and is a must for all producers of consumer goods as well as consumer organisations.

To

the helpful and supportive people of the cities of
Portsmouth, USA and Portsmouth, UK

and in particular to

Liz Binnall
Beatrice Marconi and Family
Val and Mike Verlander

Acknowledgments

For contributions, inspiration, comments and support, grateful thanks are due to:

Liz Binnall
Jan Falkowski
Wes Hart (Portsmouth University Fitness Department)
Steve and Jenette Lloyd
Pupils and teachers of Lyndhurst School, Portsmouth
Vic Palmer
Brian Pilcher (Musto)
Joe Poulter (Yamaha)
Anita Rose (Cancer Care Society)
Richard Spicer (Royal Naval & Royal Albert Yacht Club, Portsmouth)
Tim Wilks (Ribtec)
Jerry Wilson (IMS)

Also to:

Martin Critchley
for the use of his account of the Round Britain event;

The News (Portsmouth, UK)
for agreeing to let the author wring all useful information from their
coverage of the event, which was written by Mike Allen, Bernard Cole,
Martha Roberts and Matt Roper, but mostly by Jonathan Smith;

IPC International Syndication
for permission to use the article by Denis O'Neill
which first appeared in 'Motor Boat and Yachting'.

Photographs are courtesy of
Jan Falkowski, Tony Holkham, Keith Poole and Mike Verlander.

Above all, the author wishes to express his thanks to

Alan Priddy

who has shown great patience and amazing recall over many months
while we have been weaving together the thousands of pieces comprising
Beating the Big One..

CONTENTS   Page

Foreword by DAG PIKE   8

Introduction   10

1	1990 : Round Scotland	12
2	1992 : Round Britain	15
3	1993 : Round Ireland	32
4	1996 : Biscay	37
5	Atlantic Challenge	41
6	The crew — the right stuff	53
7	The team that stayed behind	57
8	The right equipment	61
9	The sponsors, supporters and beneficiaries	70
10	Countdown	75
11	Fit and ready?	76
12	It's too late to back out now	80
13	Leg One : New Hampshire to Nova Scotia	84
14	Leg Two : Nova Scotia to Labrador	89
15	Leg Three : Labrador to Greenland	92
16	Leg Four : Greenland to Iceland	107
17	Leg Five : Iceland to England	116
18	Follow That	125

Index   128

Foreword

The Atlantic has been a testing ground for hundreds of years. It's easy to picture the faith needed to make the first crossings, not knowing what lay at the other end. Once the initial discoveries had been made, the Atlantic became the challenge, the barrier which had to be crossed before exploration could continue. As familiarity with the Atlantic and its often treacherous ways grew, the ocean liners opened up regular routes, linking the New World with the old.

Today the giant Atlantic liners no longer ply the oceans. They have been replaced by aircraft which make the journey commonplace, but the challenge of the Atlantic remains and it is smaller craft which now set the pace. We established a new standard of Atlantic crossings back in 1986 when we set a new record in Virgin Atlantic Challenger, but even with that exciting crossing, we did not share the intimacy of the ocean which was the lot of Alan Priddy and his crew in their rigid inflatable.

To cross the Atlantic in what is virtually an open boat is a tremendous achievement. It's what the Vikings did over 1000 years ago and it hasn't got any easier. I have crossed the Atlantic in many types of craft from sail boats to cargo ships and it never gets any easier. There is a tremendous sense of achievement when you complete the crossing, but when you set out you don't want to think of the 3000 miles or so which lie ahead. You can't contemplate the enormity of what you are trying to do and you think only in the short term rather than the long term of the whole crossing. It is the only way you can cope.

It is the mental challenge which really hurts on the Atlantic. Even in Virgin Atlantic Challenger the thought of the pain and anguish we would have to endure was bad enough. The reality was a lot worse, and when you think about Alan and his crew in their tiny boat, I cannot even begin to picture the mental torture they must have endured.

The thought of giving up and putting into port is almost overwhelming at times. You would give almost anything to stop, but then on reflection you know you have to answer your conscience afterwards, so you keep going a bit longer. Then there is the rest of the crew. No one wants to be the first to suggest giving up, so you keep going. Even when a rational opportunity offered itself to give up, the team kept going and finally won through.

The Challenge becomes tougher when you have to put into harbour to refuel. It's the hardest thing in the world to climb back into the boat when you have touched the security of the shore, the welcome warmth and the hot food and drink. This is where you have to pluck up what seems to be the last resources of your courage and keep going.

I have seen the Atlantic in all its moods. There are times when it looks so benign and inviting; there are times when it unleashes its full fury. Alan had to cope with the full range of Atlantic moods and also with ice. It is a lonely place out there when you are hundreds of miles from land and the elements seem intent on destroying you. The will to keep going has to be extremely strong not to succumb to the temptations of calling it a day and calling for help.

What pleases me a great deal about this Atlantic venture is that it was done in a rigid inflatable. I was involved in developing the world's first rigid inflatables over 30 years ago when I was working with the RNLI. We thought we had achieved something special with this new type of boat, but we never envisioned it crossing the Atlantic. The rigid inflatable is a quite remarkable craft, producing levels of seaworthiness and security which are rarely found in conventional craft. Alan's crossing of the Atlantic only serves to reinforce my view that the rigid inflatable is one of the most seaworthy and safe craft ever built.

However, the best boat in the world is not much use without a crew of matching calibre. When I first heard about Alan's planned trip I felt a sense of envy. It has always been one of my ambitions to make the Atlantic crossing by rigid inflatable, but this is not an old man's sport. This was a trip for the young, or reasonably young, who are much better able to cope with the physical hardship which is part of a journey of this nature. The Atlantic is a tough testing ground, one where you need to plan the journey in detail but where you can always expect the unexpected. Alan and his crew got their share.

The team succeeded against all the odds. This Atlantic crossing was never going to be easy and the torturous route up into northern

latitudes necessitated by the need to find fuel did not make it any easier. I salute Alan and his crew who had the courage to dare and the will to succeed. The epic journey recounted in these pages is a tribute to tenacity and perseverance, of man's ability to cope with the extremes of nature and win through.

I recommend it as essential reading for all those who go down to the sea in ships (and boats).

DAG PIKE

Introduction

I first met Alan Priddy (intriguingly in the light of later events) at a commemorative *Titanic* dinner at the home of some mutual friends a few years ago. My wife, who had been a fencer until she could no longer wield the sledge hammer (only joking, Suzy), challenged Alan to a thigh-wrestling contest and won, establishing a common wavelength which on the scale of sanity was decidedly nearer the lower end. In the intervening years I have followed Alan's exploits on the water with admiration and not a little envy.

Having always loved the sea myself, but usually from the shore or the deck of a ferry, when Alan asked me to write this book my immediate thought was that I may have been one of the least qualified people to undertake such a project. I had never been in a fast power boat, let alone a RIB; I had never operated a Yamaha engine or worn a Musto suit. I don't believe until I visited the dentist recently I had ever looked at a copy of Motor Boat and Yachting. But Alan asked me to do it because I'm a writer, and he isn't. He's the first to admit that. He is an adventurer. His RIB exploits have spanned the last seven years, and it's fallen to me — happily, I must add — to tell you about it.

As a writer, my job is to gather all the information I possibly can about Alan and his crew of Jan Falkowski, Steve Lloyd and Vic Palmer — their background, the equipment they're going to use, the places they're going to visit, the people who have helped them and the people they are going to help, and put it all together into something interesting and entertaining. That's never easy when inevitably some of the plans made are made at the last minute, and other plans made go wrong, and perhaps the most difficult thing to explain is why they wanted to do it at all. But I mustn't go on about my problems in putting this book together, because this book is about Alan Priddy, and principally about his trans-Atlantic Challenge, trail-blazing a new, high latitude route through the ice from Portsmouth, New Hampshire, to Portsmouth, Hampshire, via Labrador, Greenland, Iceland and Ireland. Not just a first for this century, but for the millennium. Eric the Viking was the last to do it and, as you will read, did so under a certain amount of duress, whereas Alan did it by choice.

When Alan announced the challenge of making a high latitude crossing of the Atlantic, most people thought he was mad to even think about it — a 4100 mile journey across some of the world's most unpredictable and treacherous waters. But Alan has confidence in his own ability as a seaman, and above all as a meticulous planner. C. S. Forester, another man fascinated by the maritime world, said that the lucky man knows how much to leave to chance, and if that is true, Alan makes his own luck with a quiet determination and the ability always to keep an eye on the ultimate objective. These ingredients are what makes adventure and heroism and, in this case, I hope, a very good read.

I have already mentioned *Titanic*, and dentists, and I'll try not to mention them again, but I must tell you one of my favourite jokes, even though you've almost certainly heard it before. It concerns a man who has recently (it is 1996) been to the dentist, and has had to wait for treatment. When he finally gets home, his wife asks: "How did you get on?" "No problem," he replies, "but isn't it awful about that *Titanic*?"

It leaves me wondering whether, in the year 2065, someone in a dentist's waiting room (if such a thing exists then) will pick up a copy of Motor Boat and Yachting and read for the first time about Alan Priddy's exploits in a RIB. Somehow I doubt it. He is already making his mark, and I would put money on his being a household name before very long. He already is, among power boaters in the Portsmouth area, and his fame is spreading. How that fame came about is a long story, but one well worth telling, and as the adventures get bigger and bigger as the 90s progress towards the millennium, you will gain some insight into what drives Alan Priddy and his team to bolder and bolder things.

Beating the Big One has something for everyone. You can sit in an armchair and relive the storms, ice, stress, exhilaration and achievement of Alan and his crew in the comfort of your own home and marvel at their success; you can determine to get out on the water yourself and see what it's really like out there in the elements (you can include me in this group); you can decide to go the whole hog and go out and buy a RIB and go on some adventures for yourself, on any of the several of the routes described in this book; or, if you're already a boat owner, maybe you want to have a go at beating The Big One yourself. Alan, Jan, Steve and Vic did it, and are waiting to hear from someone else who can maybe do it quicker; there are a number of ways in which you could better Alan Priddy — except being the first. No one can take that away from him. What I hope you, the reader, will take away is the knowledge that in these days of economic uncertainty, social upheaval and technological chaos is that there are still heroes. And heroes are meant to be followed.

So if this heart-warming and exciting story shames you into daring to cross the Solent in broad daylight under somebody else's steam, I guess that's something. But many, I hope, will be inspired to far greater things.

Tony Holkham, Chichester, November 1997

ONE : 1990 : ROUND SCOTLAND

Inverness to Inverness round Scotland via Caledonian Canal

This summer, twenty one days after leaving Portsmouth, New Hampshire, the 7.5 metre rigid inflatable boat (RIB) *Spirit of Portsmouth* was winched ashore in Old Portsmouth, Hampshire, having made a daring high latitude crossing of the Atlantic Ocean. Few can imagine what it took to achieve such a feat, so this book has been written to tell you. A great deal of preparation went into this adventure, and we are going to start from the very beginning.

The crew of *Spirit of Portsmouth*, Alan Priddy, Jan Falkowski, Steve Lloyd and Vic Palmer have been partners in sporting events for 15 years and some originally raced off-road vehicles against each other. Their previous small craft achievements (not necessarily together, but all involving Alan Priddy) include:

June 1990: The Round Scotland event saw a 15-foot RIB start to break up in heavy seas off John O'Groats. Vic Palmer held the component parts together for the last 80 miles.

June 1992: The record for Round Britain by RIB was secured by a single, unchanged crew, taking just 89.5 hours to complete the circuit. The weather was so bad in the North Sea that an official on board as an observer spent much of the 330 miles on his knees praying for deliverance.

August 1993: A circuit of Ireland was completed, starting and finishing in Bangor. Alan was one of four skippers on the 800 mile trip. The weather hindered them every mile of the way with apparent wind speeds over 50 knots. In the Atlantic, the RIB hit a whale, but despite this and other adventures, another record was set at just over 44 hours.

September 1995: A record-setting "bridge" of small boats linking Hurst Castle to the Isle of Wight was organised for Children in Need.

June 1996: The trans-Atlantic crew raced the ferry from Bilbao to Portsmouth. The ferry won, but only just. The voyage took just 33 hours.

March 1997: Another record for circumnavigating the Isle of Wight six times in 24 hours. Much of the night was spent sheltering from heavy seas in Yarmouth Bay.

And finally The Big One. All of these events will be described in the following pages. But before we go any further, and certainly before you read about Alan Priddy's exploits in full, let me tell you what it's like riding up front in Alan Priddy's RIB, in case you don't know.

As we set out into a six foot sea at about 25 knots, I am put in mind of a mouse on a bouncy castle with a party of three-year-olds. Because the waves are irregular sizes (about 4 to 8 feet from trough to crest) and distances apart, it is difficult to gauge what the boat is going to do as it crosses each one at speed — sometimes the bow lifts high out of the water, giving a momentary feeling of weightlessness; sometimes there is a surging forward followed by a heavy thud as the boat hits the next wave flat, and the world shudders and you bang your knees on the console. Some ancient words spring to your lips just before you know it's going to happen again. And again. And again. Alan's advice is to relax, so you try, but you cannot quite bring yourself to release your vice-like grip on the bar in front of you. It's not so bad if you keep your knees slightly bent, but that only brings them closer to the console. Sometimes your feet come out of the straps and the only contact you have with the boat is your grip on the bar. The Nab Tower gets no closer, and with the wind roaring in your ears, Alan reminds you that this is 'calm', and as the coastline quickly disappears in the low cloud that visibility is 'good'. Compared with the North Atlantic, that is. There is no horizon, just the constant waves coming towards you at frightening speed, grey and featureless. Alan tells you that in the North Atlantic, you wouldn't see the Tower until you were right up to it. That's what it's like against the tide.

With the tide, the motion is different. There is more surfing, and periods of steady progress, but then the boat skims off the top of a wave and there isn't another to take its place, so you crash down into a trough, every bone in your body vibrating.

Once round the Tower, with the wind behind you, it is quieter, and you can converse after a fashion. The coast is invisible, and even this close to home you have to rely on the compass. We are less than two miles from shore before we see any sign of it. I am ready to get off this fairground ride now. I can't imagine what it's like to do this in bad weather, in freezing weather, in foggy weather, with ice about, but I have been allowed a glimpse of the motion and the physical strength needed to cope with it. I try not to think about what a 60 foot wave looks like.

Hayling Island is a welcome sight and I know that in another 10 minutes I might well have been sick. I fail to see how anyone can put up with this treatment for hours, let alone days at a time. And keep watch. And navigate. I can barely bring myself to look to one side, and after just an hour I am feeling queasy, bruised and thoroughly disorientated. Back on land, I recall the ride as if it had been a dream. Up front is probably the place where the motion is worst. There are more comfortable seats further aft, where you feel safer, and in the right circumstances, that is dead tired, you might be able to snatch a little sleep.

In days long past, when Alan Priddy was a child, it was possible to make a canoe out of a deck chair, dam a stream running at the bottom of your garden, and boat all year round. A vivid imagination would do the rest. In 1989, Alan saw an advertisement for a RIB race around Scotland, and went straight out and bought a brand new boat. He fitted two 40hp engines, and waited eagerly for the day to come.

'The Highlands and Islands RIB Race' was first conceived by the organisers as a 'cruise in company'. It quickly developed keen interest from many racing competitors, some of whom even built special boats for the event. The course was a circular one, starting and finishing in Inverness, and took in the Caledonian Canal, the Western Isles, and the whole of the north of Scotland.

The endurance style of the competition, with a series of relatively long legs, appealed to Alan's sense of adventure. It was a test of seamanship and navigation as much as a test of boats. One of the problems for Alan particularly was the overall logistics of competing a long way from home. The long trail north, towing a ton and a half of boat, plus a support vehicle for fuel and spares, then the hotel accommodation for all the crew at each stop, would need some organising. It was also a frightening prospect to contemplate the average 100 mile legs — Alan remembers wondering how anyone could endure that sort of punishment in the open sea in a small boat.

The weather turned out to be very kind, and the contestants were able to enjoy the magnificent scenery on route, which itself inspired more than one of the contestants to seek new challenges and visit new places. Some firm friendships made during the event have endured — it was during this event that Alan met Jan Falkowski — and many still keep in touch, and still talk about the event. The fact that Alan's boat fell apart on the finishing line did not deter him from wanting to find more adventures.

The event was held again in 1991 with most of the original entrants taking part. It was the start of a long learning process which would land Alan Priddy in the pack ice off the coast of Greenland. In 1991, he was still blissfully unaware of where that process was to lead.

TWO : 1992 : ROUND BRITAIN

The following is based on the account kindly provided by Martin Critchley —

Background

The Round Britain RIB Challenge came from the simple suggestion that, instead of taking the boat up by road for the Round Scotland run, taking the boat up by sea actually constituted half the course of a Round Britain event. There was a growing interest in the current record for a non-stop circumnavigation set by the Royal Marines at 90 hours. The Marines' record was for boats under 50 feet, and was set at the relatively slow pace of 17 knots, achieved with a relay crew. For them, it was only the boat that completed the whole tour.

There had been various challenges to the Marines, notably by the Sea Cadets, but without success. The Royal Engineers (REME) at Marchwood were keen to challenge the Marines' record. In a chance meeting with Alan Priddy, the format of the 1992 event was conceived to be run with overnight stops, as an event in its own right, and as a feasibility exercise for a non-stop attempt in 1993. In the meantime, an overall organisation for RIBs had been formed — The British Inflatable Boat Owners Association (BIBOA), with Alan Priddy on its competition committee. There was clearly a growing interest in RIBs and RIB racing. In parallel with all this, Marina Developments Limited (MDL), the owners of some of Britain's best marinas, were anxious to promote a Round Britain event to support their marina activities. Richard Reddyhoff at MDL issued a challenge to beat the Marines' record.

In the end, all these various strands came together to become the Round Britain RIB Challenge 1992, and there was a general belief that, with the right weather, the Marines' record could be reduced to 75 hours. Martin Critchley was appointed team manager, with Alan Priddy technical manager and Jan Falkowski as medical officer. There were six entries:

BOAT	ENGINES	SKIPPER	BOAT NAME
Ribtec 700	2x100 Mercury	J-P Waroux	*Solent One*
Ribtec 700	2x90 Yamaha	A Priddy	*Never Enough*
Ribtec 645	1x200 Mariner	J Falkowski	*The Shrink*
Avon 5 metre	1x90 Johnson	S Lawson	*Salty Sam*
Ring 22/Chinook	1x200 Mariner	T Budd	*69*
Delta 7.7	2xXR2 Mercury	B Glicksberg	*Riba*

Logistics

The Challenge would not be a cheap affair and, as well as entrants' individual sponsors, Solent Challengers Limited, BIBOA and Marina Developments Limited supported the event. In broad terms, the replacement value of a typical 6 to 7 metre RIB is approximately £30,000, divided equally between the hull and the engines. All the boats in the Challenge had outboard engines (although there already were in existence excellent RIBs designed for offshore work with inboard engines, both petrol and diesel, driving through stern drives and water jets).

A GPS (Global Positioning System) Navigation receiver, which played a major part in the Challenge and is recommended for any boat undertaking serious offshore work, represents a cost of £1-2,000.

Dry suits for crew protection have developed from diving practice. Modern suits for boating use were proofed fabric with rubber neck and wrist seals. They were, within reasonable limits, comfortable to wear and essential for protection from spray and wind chill. Suits cost between £250 and 300 each.

Other than the 5 metre Avon, which was substantially smaller than the remainder of the fleet and only carried a single 90 hp motor, the boats were all able to provide around 200 hp, whether in a single or twin motor installation. It was not surprising, therefore, that the petrol consumption of the boats should be similar at approximately 2 miles per gallon. Petrol was bought at forecourt prices rather than marina prices (which are consistently higher), the price paid being around £2.20 per gallon. Maths graduates will realise that the unit cost is just over £1.00 per mile per boat — rounded up, £2,000 per boat for the full course. To this had to be added the cost of 20 gallons of 2-stroke oil for each boat, say another £400. In practical terms, the maximum fuel capacity for one boat was about 150 gallons, divided between standard tanks, additional long-range tanks and emergency flexible tanks. Any additional fuel storage would become a problem due to the volume within the boat, and the dead weight at the start of the leg. Allowing a reasonable safety margin, 200 mile legs between fuel stops were a sensible range, and this range determined the voyage plan for the Challenge.

Shore Party

An event like the Round Britain Challenge, particularly with petrol-engined boats, either individually or in a fleet, cannot be considered without land-based support parties. A larger diesel boat with accommodation on board should manage unaided with diesel fuel readily available in most ports. For the six boats in the 1992 Challenge fleet, there was a substantial shore party serving the combined fleet. This was partly the approach of the REME entry who treated the Challenge as an operational exercise, and partly a feasibility test for the overall organisation for a future attempt on a non-stop run round Britain.

The full shore party was composed of:—

[1] 5 ton Bedford Truck — 50 jerry cans of 20 litres each, outboard motor spares, 2-stroke oil; general support of the boats.

[2] 5 ton Bedford Truck — Field tents, camp kitchen, rations, sleeping bags, etc.; general support of the shore party.

[3] Land Rover Defender — General support and reconnaissance; used for towing the boat trailer in emergencies.

[4] Vauxhall Frontera 4x4 — Loaned by Vauxhall Motors to the Challenge, the quickest and most comfortable of the shore vehicles; designated for the film crew, it was more than useful in general support, and was used for urgent errands like sourcing spare motor parts.

[5] Sherpa Panel Van — Loaned with a pair of drivers by Royal Mail, this vehicle carried spare clothes and personal effects of all the boat crews; it was also a welcome provider of hot drinks in times of stress. The Sherpa crew kept their own log of the event. They clocked up 2747 miles, half as much again as the boat crews, of which the longest run was 394 miles from Holyhead to Oban. They made all the landfall stops except Ramsgate, and even managed goodwill visits to one or two local sorting offices on their way round. The van, diesel-engined, returned a creditable 30.1 mpg for the event.

Day 1 : Friday, 29 May 1992
Southampton - Penzance
183 miles

The competing boats had spent the night at Hythe Marina Village, and on the Friday morning the fleet made the short crossing of Southampton Water to Ocean Village for the pre-race press conference. A small crowd of well-wishers, onlookers and passers-by mingled with the video cameras of TVS, the reporters of the Southampton Echo, and our own video crew sponsored by JVC to record the event. Finally all the interviews were completed. The crews kitted up and moved their boats out to the Start Line off the Royal Yacht Squadron at the head of Southampton Water. There was a ten minute flare, then a five minute gun. The last seconds were counted down, and at 10 am the six boats were off on their 1800 mile adventure, roaring down Southampton Water together, leaving the wide expanse of the channel filled with churning foam.

The two quicker boats, the Chinook *69* and the Belgian *Riba* broke away from the main fleet and pushed ahead in almost perfect conditions. There was no wind; yacht sails hung limp in the air, and the water was mirror calm. The remainder of the fleet made their rendezvous at the Needles, waved goodbye to the support boats and set a course westwards for Penzance.

The morning's run was largely uneventful, apart from a plastic bag collected around a propeller of *Never Enough*, which was soon removed. Then, just before Start Point, 90 miles into the journey, the petrol pump on the Avon Searider *Salty Sam* failed. Time and effort were spent trying to effect a repair at sea, but it proved impossible; there was no alternative but to take the crew members aboard the other boats, and take the Searider in tow. The Belgian crew of *Solent One* undertook the tow for the remaining 90 miles of the leg to Penzance. They made good time at a steady 25 knots, but at a heavy price in additional fuel consumption. Twice they ran dry, and had to be transfused with extra fuel from spare cans in the other boats. Had this been a longer leg with tighter fuel limits, it could well have been a serious problem.

The fleet swept into Penzance harbour at 7 pm to a warm welcome at the Penzance Sailing Club. The crew of the Chinook were already ensconced in the bar, having arrived at 3.40 pm followed by *Riba* at 4 pm. Overnight *Salty Sam* changed the petrol pump that had caused the problems, and they were all ready for the second leg to Holyhead.

Day 2 : Saturday, 30 May
Penzance - Holyhead
220 miles

The start was scheduled for 6 am, which seemed to catch most teams unawares. It was postponed to 6.30 am, at which time *Never Enough*, *Solent One* and *Salty Sam* put out to sea in calm conditions. The rest of the fleet struggled away at 7 am. The weather was almost ideal, with no wind and the early morning sun burning off the mist.

Once clear of Land's End, they said goodbye to England, and settled down for the long run northwards to St David's Head. The mist became more persistent and they were glad of the GPS to find their way. After a couple of hours in the mist, the leaders stopped for a comfort break and heard the late starters overtake them in the gloom two miles to the east. They settled back into the long slog northwards, the GPS guiding them to the lighthouse at St David's, which eventually loomed out of the greyness. For those used to sailing in the busy Solent waters, the Irish Sea was surprisingly empty. Not a sailing yacht to be seen anywhere, no fishing boats, no ferries, just one or two merchant vessels heading up the Bristol Channel which were also soon lost in the mist.

North of St David's the morning calm was replaced by a short chop, a surprise with so little wind. The only breakage of the day was unfortunately *Salty Sam* again, when the "A" frame at the rear of the boat sheared off at one mounting and subsequently collapsed, taking with it the radio aerial. The rest of the journey to Holyhead became a tiresome chore as they bucked through the waves. Once again the GPS homed them in, and they swept round the point into the welcome calm of Holyhead harbour.

It had been a long day — nearly twelve hours on the water, The crews were beginning to understand what an endurance event was all about. After refuelling the boats, the crews refuelled themselves, and took advantage of an early night ready for another 6 am start and the run north to Scotland.

Day 3 : Sunday, 31 May
Holyhead - Oban
209 miles

An early start had been scheduled for the day, which as it transpired was just as well. The slower boats set out from Holyhead at 6.30 am in an untidy following sea. They set a direct course up the Irish Sea, close to the coast of Northern Ireland, and on to Mull of Kintyre. The Chinook left at 7 am. *Riba* had transom problems and left later.

The main fleet were experiencing deteriorating conditions in the Irish Sea, with the confused following seas developing uncomfortable 2 metre waves. The Chinook made slow progress in these conditions, which did not suit its racing hull, and by chance caught up with the main fleet at 10.30 am. It was days like that, when the sea was cold, grey and unrelieved, that they were glad not to be career sailors. It was also easy to see why the Navies of the world painted their ships grey for concealment. Even the little fleet's brightly-coloured craft were soon lost in the mist and the spray.

At midday, life became more than interesting. The primary electric circuits on *Salty Sam* failed and progress under power was impossible. Repeated submerging of the little boat in the backs of the waves had taken its toll. The boats were somewhere near the Irish coast, unseen in the mist; the support crews were many miles away on the mainland. The only sensible solution was a tow across the Irish Sea to Stranraer, where help could be summoned.

This turned out to be easier said than done. *Solent One*, who had towed *Salty Sam* on the first day, was unable to manage the pull with the heavy seas, and with a full fuel load for the long leg to Oban. Her steep-pitched propellers meant that the engines were constantly overheating when towing. The tow was then swapped to *Never Enough* which, with shorter pitch props, and all spare cargo and spare crew distributed among the other boats, was able to complete the long trek into Stranraer.

In Stranraer an electrician was found, a taxi was chartered to fill up the flexible tanks from a local filling station, and the luxury of lunch was taken. Eventually at 4 pm the fleet left Stranraer as the Seacat swept in on its inaugural run to the cheers of a large crowd on the quayside.

As the boats cleared Stranraer the wind had died down, the sun had burned off the mist, and in a fine clear evening good and steady progress was made up to the Mull of Kintyre. Here the sea conditions off the point, with wind over tide, had brought up the overfalls to an alarming degree. The small boats handled these difficult conditions surprisingly well, all of them submerging themselves in the waves at some stage. There was nothing else for it but to hold their breath and wait to emerge the other side, hoping all the kit was secured. The Chinook must take the record for the number of submarine attempts — its crew made painfully slow progress and were well relieved to clear the overfalls.

Thereafter it was a smooth and clear run all the way, through magnificent scenery and warm evening sunshine to Oban. It was just short of 10 in the evening when the boats arrived. *Riba*, in the meantime, following her late start, had made steady progress without the sightseeing diversion to Stranraer, and had been comfortably berthed on the pontoon since 4.30 pm.

Another day was over. Aching muscles and bronzed faces were marking the time at sea. The camaraderie and stresses of the various crew members within the fleet were all becoming apparent, along with a collective identity and a pride in the achievement at having got so far.

The prospect for the next day was comforting, with a lunchtime start for the relatively short run up to Ullapool, where they would catch up with the Round Scotland RIB Race. In the meantime there was news that Tom Henderson was about to set out from Penzance on a single boat attempt at the non-stop round Britain record, set by the Royal Marines at 90 hours. If he was to be successful, we calculated he would pass us at Ullapool.

Day 4 : Monday, 1 June
Oban - Ullapool
110 miles

This was very much the sightseeing day of the event. The weather was glorious — bright summer sunshine, clear blue sky, and just a hint of breeze to dapple the surface of the lochs. Sadly, *Riba* had blown a gearbox on one of her Mercury XR2 motors and retired at Oban. *Salty Sam*'s crew had been unable to fix the rogue electrics in their control panel; their support crew had gone off in pursuit of a set of remote controls to reactivate the boat, while the boat crew boarded *Never Enough* to continue the Challenge.

Thus it was that only four boats left Oban for a tour of the Western Isles. The most direct route from Oban to Ullapool is 110 miles, which was ignored in favour of a southerly course round Mull to Fionnphort, the embarkation point for the island of Iona. Here there was surprise at the touring coaches and ice cream stalls of the tourists, which were a gaudy contrast to the natural beauty of the hills. A gentle stop was made for a light lunch, and then off north-eastward to Ardnamurchan.

The notorious headland at Ardnamurchan seemed innocent enough as the fleet passed by. It was then a straight heading all the way up to Loch Alsh, past the rugged grandeur of the islands of Muck and Eigg, past Mallaig, where one has to admire the railway engineers who brought the railway down to the quayside.

After Kyle of Lochalsh it was straight up the Inner Sound, where the wind had picked up a little from the north to give a light chop. The boats took it on the nose and pushed on due north. It was late afternoon as the fleet moved into the open waters of the Minch. Here the wind died away into a slightly misty evening, making the mountains and headlands look like so many cardboard cut-outs, layered off into the distance. The little fleet swung round into Ullapool harbour, four abreast in fine style, to be greeted by the assembled boats of the Scotland RIB Race, who had arrived earlier in the day.

Altogether on the day, 190 miles had been covered without fault or mishap. Complaints from the crews had died away, partly because they were getting used to the long sea days, and partly because complaints were ignored anyway. In terms of endurance events they were also learning the advantages of maintaining a steady pace throughout, being more effective than bursts of speed followed by periods of recuperation. They also considered the wisdom of *Riba* using light-weight racing engines on a heavy boat, and pushing them hard for long hours.

Similar problems had beset the RIB race fleet, with a catalogue of mechanical problems, split hulls and separating tubes due to dashing through the Scottish waters in lightly built boats. There was solid satisfaction with the round Britain fleet's own efforts, however, having covered over 800 miles, nearly half way round, and still going strong.

Day 5 : Tuesday, 2 June
Ullapool - Scrabster
98.5 miles

At exactly 11 am the RIB Race fleet shot away from Ullapool under heavy grey skies, turning the grey waters of the loch white for a few moments. The weather was force 4, forecast to die down later.

Overnight, the support for *Salty Sam* had re-rigged the electrics and got the little Avon back into a seaworthy condition. With our fleet back up to five, we were all comfortable back in our own boats. The forecast was right, for as the boats left at midday, the wind was dropping and the cloud was breaking up to ease the journey north towards Cape Wrath and the halfway point of the journey.

The sun even shone, and the fleet stopped at the Old Man of Stewart for a photo call. Then it was on to Cape Wrath itself, impressive in its scale and grandeur, and for the size of the swells which rolled around the base of the cliffs. Sea birds were everywhere, gulls, puffins, terns, gannets, wheeling and diving all around, singly and in flocks. Quite why they should gather there in particular was a mystery, but there they were, the only sign of life on the stark cliffs.

The journey was now eastwards across the top of Scotland. Progress was frustrated by a series of minor breakdowns which slowed the pace. The only disadvantage of travelling as a cruising fleet is that when one stops, all stop, and the average speed is reduced by the stopping time of all vessels. Worst plagued was *The Shrink*, where the electrics to the engine hydraulics failed and the whole boat became "live". Then a split petrol pipe caused problems which had repercussions for the rest of the day, when the tank could not be drawn from, and surplus petrol bags had to be transferred from the other boats.

Half an hour after Cape Wrath the weather started to deteriorate again, with the wind freshening from the south. The underlying swells were not the problem — it was the nasty chop on the top which the boats turned into spray, and which the cross-wind picked up and turned across the boats. Everything and everyone was being shot-blasted with salt water. There were still 40 miles to Scrabster with no alternative but to sit it out. The conditions were thoroughly uncomfortable and, despite the minor breakdowns, everyone was thankful for the underlying reliability of the engines themselves, which kept running throughout.

In the last mile the fleet overhauled a back marker from the Scotland RIB Race, limping in with a detached tube. Finally, the inner harbour at Scrabster was reached at 7.30 pm, with total relief that the saline shower was over. The halfway mark had been passed and there was a growing confidence that the Challenge might be met and the tour completed. There was even speculative talk of doing it again.

The Chinook was a new boat, based on a Ring racing hull. Tim and Gary, the crew, were learning fast about their new craft. They had tried a propeller change for the day's run with considerably improved results and sea keeping. They had rounded Cape Wrath at a much better pace and in greater comfort than their uncertain struggle around the Mull of Kintyre two days before. Doubts about their ability to complete the course were being dispelled, the other crews rooting for them to finish.

It was later learned that Tom Henderson's non-stop attempt had ended in the Irish Sea when, five hours ahead of schedule, he had struck a large floating object. The collision ripped a huge hole in the lower hull of his RIB, but fortunately missed the engine. He was able to limp on the flotation of the tubes into the Isle of Man, where his attempt was sadly abandoned.

Day 6 : Wednesday, 3 June
Scrabster - Inverness
99 miles

Wednesday morning dawned cold, grey and overcast. It was difficult to believe that midsummer's day was only three weeks away. Overnight, the crew of *The Shrink* had worked hard to remedy the faults of the previous day, and had generally tidied up all the frayed ends of a thousand miles at sea.

Once again at 11 am, the RIB Race Fleet were flagged away, off to the east, into the rain and mist. The Challenge fleet followed five minutes later at a more gentle pace. The wind was about force three on the rear three-quarter, with not much of a sea to impede progress. An hour and ten minutes from Scrabster the boats reached John o'Groats where the sea conditions changed dramatically. There was a huge swell around the point, with close set waves three metres high, superimposed from the overfalls — appalling conditions for small boats. As the Chinook struggled with this onslaught, her engine mountings gave way, and her gallant crew turned back for calmer waters and repairs. They waved the other boats on, sadly back to a fleet of four.

Once around the point, conditions were easier, and a course was set south for the first time. From here on it was homeward all the way. The wind was now square on the starboard beam, and rising to force 4. The conditions were a repeat of the previous afternoon, and thoroughly miserable. The waves were on the beam, generally about a metre high, sometimes twice that, but well-spaced and not a problem for the stability of rigid inflatable hulls. The boats readily steadied themselves as the waves passed under, and showed no signs of rolling and broaching, which can so easily happen with boats having open gunwhales.

The wind freshened to force five and it continued to rain. Raindrops sting at 30 knots, but not as much as the salt spray picked up by the cross winds. It was impossible to keep eyes open long enough to see, and goggles were covered in salt spray on both sides. The only practical protection was a diving mask, and so it was for the next three hours, struggling on in miserable silence towards Inverness. Conversation was impossible without mouthfuls of salt water, and it was a case for gritting the teeth and pushing on. Two casualties from the RIB Race were passed limping back to the cover of Scrabster.

It was no sightseeing day. The coastline was lost in the mist, and the only contact with the civilised world was the magic radio beam that steered the GPS and set the course for Inverness. Finally, the boats turned into the Moray Firth and more sheltered waters. By the final approach to the Kessock Bridge the wind had died away, and the four little boats rolled under the bridge in line abreast.

The RIB Race teams were there, talking of finishing times, and of packing up to go home. The round Britain fleet's was of refuelling, hot baths and a full day again tomorrow, down to Edinburgh. As the boats pulled away from the jetty at North Kessock to moor up for the night, it was a delight to see the lone Chinook come roaring down the Firth to catch up. The problem with the broken engine mounts had turned out to be a loose motor casing which was far from terminal. They had done well to effect a repair and recover the sea time in difficult conditions.

Day 7 : Thursday, 4 June
Inverness - Edinburgh
120 miles

By now, the whole of the event team were working well together, and the various boat and support crews had established a rapport and a purposeful camaraderie. After arriving at Inverness, the boats were safely moored at Fortrose, and all the team had a night on the town to celebrate the one thousand miles achieved to date. Thus it was that on Thursday morning everyone was a little slow off the mark.

At 12.30 pm the little fleet of five boats moved out into the Moray Firth in glorious sunshine and flat calm waters. It was calm enough for those still nursing hangovers to sleep on the floor of the boats.

The destination for the day was Port Edgar Marina at Queensferry, underneath the Forth Road Bridge 120 miles away. Back at North Kessock, the Scotland RIB Race started their next leg at 1 pm, heading for Aberdeen a mere 90 miles away. After an hour, the leaders of the race slowly drew past the Challenge fleet, all heading eastwards. Still the calm conditions prevailed, dolphins and basking seals watching with interest as the multi-coloured fleet roared by.

Passing Banff, a light northerly wind started to pick up. Soon after, the first of the day's breakdowns occurred when the gear linkage on the Chinook slipped and they lost all forward drive. It was their turn to be towed, five miles into the nearest sheltered anchorage, which turned out to be the charming little harbour at Rosehearty. Fortunately, 20 minutes later the problem was fixed and the fleet moved on eastwards and around the point, as the bombers of the USAF zoomed overhead on their practice missions. The wind freshened to force 3 or 4 as the boats turned south again; the North Sea was picking up into steady following waves a metre high.

For the first time, there was a significant amount of merchant shipping, mostly oil rig service ships working in and out of Aberdeen. The short following seas were not to the liking of the Chinook, which was taking large amounts of water over the bow and losing time. Their problems were aggravated by a bilge pump failure at this time of need. They headed for the shelter of Aberdeen and for help from the back-up crews of the RIB Race, the Challenge crews being well on the way to Edinburgh.

The remaining four boats pressed on southwards as the following waves gradually increased. They were bumping and surfing their way southwards at a steady 22 knots. Even with all the stops and interruptions an average of 21 knots had been maintained, and Edinburgh looked achievable before nightfall.

Turning westwards into the Firth of Forth, the wind turned also, and built up huge confused seas in the mouth of the estuary. The wind was force 5, straight over the tide, pushing up nine and ten metre waves. For the helmsmen it was like driving a car up the side of a house. It was difficult to give the boat enough momentum to run up the back of the waves before balancing on the crest with the propellers in the air and then rolling down the face. The skipper of *Salty Sam* suffered a nasty shock and a badly cut lip when, cresting a huge wave, his crew fell on top of him, crushing his face into the console.

The 30 miles of the Forth along to Queensferry took an eternity. Passing the oil rig construction sites, the lights on top of the Forth Road Bridge could be seen in the distance, but never seemed to come any nearer. Still bumping and surfing, crews were fatigued and quiet. Finally, after ten hours almost to the minute, it was under the bridge, round the breakwater, and into the sheltered basin of Port Edgar.

The weather forecast was not welcomed, with the prospect of more bumping and surfing to come.

After repairs at Aberdeen, the Chinook had made steady progress as far as Stonehaven, and hoped to catch up with the fleet in the morning, omitting the long detour up the Forth. The remaining boats in the Scotland RIB Race would be racing from Aberdeen down to Queensferry, but the Round Britain Challenge fleet hoped to be away to the south before they arrived.

Day 8 : Friday, 5 June
Edinburgh - Grimsby
216 miles

The weather had changed little overnight. The dawn found the wind still blowing north-easterly at force 5, the sky heavy and overcast, with gales forecast. Was this really June? The decision was made to run as far as possible before the weather closed in.

Refuelling was a daily ritual of some substance, to load upwards of 100 gallons of petrol into each boat, using a relay of jerry cans. For each boat the fuel load was about a tonne, almost equal to the weight of the boat itself. Fuelling complete, the boats left the calm of the Port Edgar basin, past the High School girls having kayak lessons, and out under the lofty structures of the Forth Bridges.

Straight away it was head into the wind and waves at force 5. Taking a little shelter on the southern shore it took an hour and a half to reach Bass Rock, with its colony of gannets, and the open expanse of the North Sea. Turning at the rock the wind was on the beam three quarter and the seas were mounting up. Heading south the conditions were becoming exciting, to say the least — waves six to ten metres high with an overlying chop of random waves a metre high. In these conditions, the design of the boats were coming into their own — the deep "V" of the lower hull gripping the waves and holding course, while the side tubes took the slam and held the roll at the tumbling crests. Surprisingly, a steady 15 knots was maintained.

As predicted, the weather deteriorated further, with reduced visibility, and the waves were now up to a frightening 12 metres high, with about 100 metres between each wave. They were big enough to allow the boats to run along the troughs and manoeuvre around the more alarming of the breaking crests, but it was becoming obvious that in these conditions Grimsby was not attainable before nightfall; even at 15 knots it would be midnight before arrival.

A wave trough conference resolved to round St Abbs Head and run for cover at Berwick on Tweed. Within just a mile of Berwick, a random wave submerged the motor of *Salty Sam* and all power was lost. Very quickly, the wind and the waves were driving the helpless little boat on to the sand bar north of the harbour entrance. With the waves crashing with awesome power, suddenly it was an emergency rescue situation.

Never Enough was the nearest of the bigger RIBs, while *Solent One* was struggling with a sheared steering cotter, and life was becoming very serious. With *Salty Sam* only two wave lengths from the destructive surf, *Never Enough* beat a careful path back up wind, climbing the cliff-like faces of the waves, to work back to the little boat's position.

There was only one chance to come close enough to secure a line before both boats were in danger. A line was thrown across, and after some scrambled knotting a tow secured. Inching across the waves, the boats pulled out to sea, away from the desperate conditions on the sand bar. The rope was too short for effective towing — if any rope would have been effective in those conditions. At times, the two boats were hanging on opposite sides of the same wave, with only the line stopping them both falling into the troughs.

Slowly and carefully, the boats manoeuvred towards the Berwick Harbour wall. It took an age as they balanced their way across the waves, creeping towards safety. Finally, they made it, threading a way up the unfamiliar but well-marked channel to the security of the dock basin.

Emergency repairs were effected and an event briefing held in a local café. The forecast indicated the storm blowing out overnight, but in the meantime visibility had deteriorated considerably — the only sensible course was to stay there, telephone the support crews to wait at Grimsby, and hope to make an early start in the morning to catch them up by lunchtime. It was beginning to look as if the Challenge was going to be more challenging than some participants had thought.

Day 9 : Saturday, 6 June
Berwick upon Tweed - Lowestoft
330 miles

At ten past four on a cold, grey morning, the little fleet pulled out of Berwick. Morale was low, to say the least. They should have been way to the south in Grimsby and, with only two days and 700 miles to go, they felt lonely, hungry, isolated and a long, long way from home.

The wind had moderated a little overnight, although there was still a large swell running, with nine metre waves and poor visibility. With a more generous schedule, they would have waited, but as it was there was no alternative but to push on. Relying totally on the GPS, a course was set out to sea, past Holy Island, unseen in the mist. Then through the inner sound at the Farne Islands, where all that could be seen was a sand bank and a few rocks through the swirling clouds.

Progress was at a steady 20 knots in grim silence, wondering what the normal world was up to on this Saturday morning. The heavy seas and slow progress had taken their toll, and it was becoming doubtful if any of the boats would have enough fuel to reach the scheduled stop at Grimsby. There would have to be refuelling in between. In innocent optimism, the fleet pulled into the yellow-stained but sheltered waters of the Tees, and up to Port Clarence at Middlesbrough. The Harbour Master was found under the old transporter bridge, as were four small boats, big ships, big cranes, big chimneys — but no petrol.

There was nothing for it but to put back into the rolling swell of the North Sea and head on to Whitby, where there was rumoured to be petrol at the marina. Tanks were getting low, but steady progress was made until Runswick Bay, where *Salty Sam* stopped to tip an emergency jerry can into the main tank and failed to restart. It was another tow, unceremoniously, into Whitby. *Salty Sam* was continuing to experience electrical problems. In a quayside conference it was resolved that the boat should be left at Whitby, but its crew would continue on the other boats in the hope of completing the Challenge, making better time for the remaining legs.

Petrol was not in fact available at Whitby Marina, although there was a filling station directly opposite the quay in the old basin. It was possible to hump the flexible tanks up the quay wall and take on enough fuel to head south, although reaching Grimsby was still doubtful. The road crews were telephoned to back-track and meet at Scarborough for refuelling. Maybe even lunch. The day was not going well.

Just three boats left charming Whitby, with its brightly coloured fishing boats, once more into the North Sea. Morale dropped to new depths. *Salty Sam* was out of the Challenge, the fleet was late, and the organisation was falling apart. The compensating factor was the clearing mist and the Yorkshire coast slipping by without further incident.

Creeping into the shelter of Scarborough harbour, the crews were taken aback by the berthing master, who suggested that motor boats could not be admitted without the prior written consent of the Harbour Master. Fortunately, logic and circumstance prevailed, and the boats were admitted. A much warmer welcome then followed from a lady diver who invited our heroes to the Scarborough Diving Club for lunch. Their warm hospitality filled an hour until the road crew arrived to start refuelling.

The weather forecast was not good, and it was tempting to stay in Scarborough among friends. But if there was to be any chance of reaching Southampton on Sunday evening — the next day — further progress would have to be made that afternoon. The forecast was for a north-easterly storm coming through, although immediately the wind had dropped and the sea was calm in the afternoon sunshine. It was decided to run ahead of the weather, and chance an evening run across Bridlington Bay and the Humber Estuary to the Norfolk coast. The shore party were sent ahead to Cromer, and the boats set out with the dark clouds on the far horizon.

The Coastguard radioed a stern warning as the boats picked their way through a forest of fishermen's pots. An hour later, the storm struck. The Coastguard had been right in every detail — the wind was the top of force 6, driving cold mist and five metre waves in every direction. Progress was violent, uncomfortable and slow, and Scarborough seemed a lifetime ago. The three remaining boats, all built by Ribtec, handled the seas superbly, although only about 12 knots was possible. The long day was becoming a stormy nightmare, and the nightmare became real as the light faded and an error was made on the GPS. They were lost somewhere off The Wash, in a storm, in the dark. Rapid progress in rough seas in the dark is a haphazard and terrifying experience for a small boat. The speed and size of the waves and their troughs cannot be seen, let alone judged. But as the final light died in the sky, the worst of the storm passed, and out of the dark loomed a marker buoy. The chance sighting gave a location 20 miles north of Blakeney.

They reached Cromer at midnight, only to find there were no harbour facilities, just a small slipway adjacent to the pier, which was impossible with the waves crashing straight on to the beach. There was no alternative — tired, battered and miserable, they had to press on in the blackness to Great Yarmouth.

In a fatigued state, with eyes red from many hours at sea, lashed by wind, salt and spray, it was difficult to pick out unfamiliar marks and buoys in the dark. The entrance to Great Yarmouth was missed, lost against the lights of the new road bridge behind. Finally, landfall was made at Lowestoft at 2.28 am. It was 22 hours since leaving Berwick.

At that late hour a Kebab shop opposite the Yacht Club was in the process of closing up. A Turkish member of *The Shrink*'s crew persuaded the proprietor to re-open and feed the fleet. Thereafter, tiredness took over and the crews slept as they were, in the car park, in their dry suits. That is how they were found in the morning, asleep under boats, under trailers, behind the stores — much to the amusement of a visiting cruise fleet of Norwegian yachtsmen.

Day 10 : Sunday, 7 June
Lowestoft - Southampton
250 miles

Following the mammoth day on Saturday, the crews awoke stiff and aching, bodies battered by long sea hours and sleeping rough. Overnight, the faithful road crews had arrived and refuelling was under way. Thanks to the unwitting hospitality of the Yacht Club, yesterday's salt was washed off, and at 8.50 am, unbreakfasted, the trio of boats departed. Amazingly, through the remaining hours of darkness, the storm had blown through, leaving the sea calm and bright.

Under these conditions there was some hope that they might still make Southampton before evening. In smooth conditions, the course was south, dodging unmarked drift nets by Sizewell Power Station to reach Orford Point in an hour. It was then straight across the Thames Estuary in eerie calm after the storms and trauma of the day before. The Thames was strangely barren, a lone scruffy puffin the only representative of Mother Nature. There were many large ships further to the east, beyond the sand banks, and a huge ship barge being towed eastwards across their course.

Speed was averaging 30 knots, and despite fatigue and a lack of breakfast, hopes continued to rise. The Kent coast reached without mishap, and Broadstairs passed, they dashed into Ramsgate for a petrol top-up and a brunch of fish and chips. Surprisingly, Ramsgate is one of the few ports on the perimeter of Britain where petrol is available on the quay; most ports have diesel for the fishermen, but very few have petrol, hence the need for any crew considering a circumnavigation with petrol-engined boats to have a refuelling party.

From Ramsgate it was going to be tight to reach Southampton for the planned reception at 5 pm. In growing excitement, they telephoned ahead and agreed an hour's postponement. Leaving Ramsgate, the boats picked their way across the sand banks in Pegwell Bay, unable to believe the total change in the weather back to summer. A school of dolphins were also enjoying the June sunshine, dipping and rolling in the Channel waters. Sweeping round the Kent coast, progress was abruptly halted when *The Shrink* collected a plastic bag around the propeller, right outside the entrance to Dover Western Docks. Fortunately the bag was soon removed and progress resumed westwards.

Past the Channel Tunnel works, it was now the home straight. The final objective was in sight as rising spirits overcame the fatigue. In the calm conditions, several crew slept in the bottom of the boats; it was noted that if any successful non-stop circumnavigation were to be achieved, crews would <u>have</u> to sleep aboard.

Beachy Head was passed in the Sunday afternoon sunshine. Sunny it might have been, but the chill factor travelling at over 30 knots was surprising, and all were still glad of the protection from the dry suits.

On through the inshore channel at Selsey, straight down the Solent, busy with Sunday yachtsmen, and up Southampton Water. At Lee-on-Solent there were the first of the welcome party — small boats out to meet us, including the little Avon *Salty Sam*, brought down by road overnight from Whitby. Well-wishers and supporters were taken aboard, and together all raced over the finish line at the Royal Yacht Squadron.

Aches and pains and lost sleep were all forgotten as they crossed the line at 5.30 pm. It was a slow and joyful procession round to Ocean Village for the press reception. They had made it. Despite the struggle at Mull of Kintyre and the monster waves in the North sea, they had made it. Despite the simple preparation and tight budget, they had made it. It was sad that the Belgian crew of *Riba* had not finished, too, and that Tim and Gary in the Chinook, after covering 1000 miles, could not share in the final glory. Nonetheless, three small boats and four crews had met, and beaten, the Challenge. The total distance covered was 1843 nautical miles at an average speed of 20.6 knots. The important thing, though, was that the total lapsed sea time was 89.5 hours. The record was theirs. But not alone — no challenging enterprise at sea can be successful without help. The Challenge, mounted by Solent Challengers Limited in conjunction with Marina Developments Limited, could not have succeeded without the considerable help and support of the following —

Automatic Transmissions • Concept Interiors • DJS Mouldings
JVC Video • Nash & Partners Architects • Royal Mail • R.E.M.E
Trimble Navigation • Valvoline Oil Company • Vauxhall Motors

Funds went to the Children's Ward, Southampton General Hospital.

THREE : 1993 : ROUND IRELAND

An introduction to the Atlantic came when Alan and his crew took on the Round Ireland voyage in 1993, where an encounter with a whale nearly spelled disaster. Circumnavigating the rugged coast of Ireland in a small open boat is not for the faint-hearted. Motor Boat and Yachting staff photographer Lester McCarthy joined a group of fearless RIBsters in their attempt to complete the 750 mile circuit in record time. Denis O'Neill tells his story:

We'd landed on Inishmore, the largest of the Aran Islands, eight miles off western Ireland's magnificent Connemara coast. It had been a hard day, but the best of the trip so far. The village of Kilronan was quiet and peaceful in the warm midsummer's evening, a welcome contrast to the noise and pounding that we had endured on the non-stop 184 mile voyage to get here, passing the dramatic islands, bays and mountains of Cork, Kerry, Clare and Galway along the way.

There was no doubt we deserved a drink. Our attempt to circumnavigate the Emerald Isle was on schedule, and the sun had at last broken through the rain and heavy cloud that had hounded us since our journey began. As we pushed open the door to the bar we were met by nothing less than total uproar. The place was packed to bursting. Through scarves and flags of green, white and gold two televisions blasted out a football commentary so loudly we could hardly hear ourselves shout for beer. Big Jack and the lads were playing Norway and needed a draw to get through to the next stage of the World Cup Finals. They duly did and we had no option but to join in the celebrations. As the smooth stout was downed we were noticed and the islanders, intrigued, were keen to hear how we'd got there.

Our adventure had begun three days earlier after two RIBs from England and one from Belgium travelled together 120 miles from Conwy in North Wales to Bangor, near Belfast, to join up with Garth Henry and the crew of *Ocean Endeavour*, a 7.4m (24ft 3in) Tornado with single Yamaha inboard diesel, from Portrush, County Londonderry, in order to fulfil a united and long-held ambition to circle Ireland.

The first two days of the attempt were, quite frankly, almost complete misery. The coastline was obscured, the sky thickly overcast, and the sea cold. Day One was especially gruelling. Although the shortest of the five legs, it was a 130 mile beat south for Wicklow into the teeth of a Force 8 gale and very heavy seas. All the boats and crew took a severe battering. Conditions were so bad I wasn't once able to even get out my camera — not that there was much worth photographing — my priority was holding on.

I was travelling with Alan Priddy in *Never Enough*, a Ribtec 700 with twin 90hp Yamahas. He and his crew of five were taking the expedition very seriously. Every task was conducted with military precision and little conversation took place on board. Hardly a word was exchanged between us that day, and even then it was only the occasional cry or curse as we bashed off the waves which were reaching nine or ten, maybe more, feet high. It was an exhausting trip made worse by having someone sitting in front of me so I couldn't watch the sea to judge the bumps and crashes.

Because we were passing so many headlands the sea was often coming at us from different directions, and a couple of times we hit some of the waves so hard the boat would stop dead. Like all the boats we were continually awash, which wasn't too much of a problem except that it threatened our dry store, and essential supplies of food like pepperoni, apples and Mars bars.

There was some seasickness that first day but the biggest problem was having salt water in our faces for hours on end. At times it could be torture, despite the various creams and lotions we applied. Everybody's eyes were bloodshot, despite a variety of eye protection. While Garth's crew had helmets with visors, most others wore snorkelling masks; a few preferred skiing shades and the Belgian, Jean-Pierre Waroux, looked rather dashing in a pair of old-fashioned motorcycle goggles.

I was kitted out in a dry suit under my offshore sailing jacket. I had no helmet, only a woollen hat under my sailing hood, and fingerless gloves to allow me to operate my camera. Wearing so much gear we found we would start to sweat getting ready, but it soon became cooler once we got out to sea.

Eight long hours later we arrived at Houth Marina in Wicklow. That night the forecast warned of south-westerly gales, which I was surprised to find did not seem to bother any of the others.

On the second day I travelled with Jean-Pierre and Karina, heading for Kinsale. Life with these two, in *Solent*, their 7m (23ft) Ribtec with a single 4.2 litre Mercruiser inboard diesel, was quite a contrast to *Never Enough*. They were in cruising mode, stopping when they felt like it for snacks and Gauloises. The best thing about being with them, though, was the abundance and superb quality of the provisions on board: they carried masses of delicatessen food, cakes, fruit and, of course, plenty of delicious Belgian chocolates. They appreciated the pleasure of just stopping and enjoying a short break — often to the bemusement of the rest of the convoy.

Thankfully the gale didn't materialise, but it was another difficult day, dull and overcast. The wind still managed to get up to Force 5 from the south-west so that it was on our nose again, and at times there was fairly dense sea mist to contend with. By midday, the grinding conditions were tiring the crews so we stopped off in Wexford for half an hour to gather our strength before carrying on. We ended up standing outside a corner cafe drinking tea in the pouring rain, not very glamorous but at least a bit of a respite.

While the others stayed close to the Waterford coast for shelter, Jean-Pierre insisted on cutting straight across from Carnsore Point. It was a really rough option, and at one point the boat took off and landed on its side so hard it cracked its bow canopy.

Taking the inshore route, though, meant the others had to keep a sharp eye out for drift nets. Two of the boats got fishing lines around their propellers and had to stop and reverse to unwind them; then, coming into Kinsale we all had to deviate a few hundred yards to avoid just one enormous net.

Kinsale, on the coast of County Cork, is a very nice fishing town but, like all the places where we stopped, we never had a chance to see much of it. We would arrive, prepare for the following day, take a shower at that night's B&B, grab some dinner, have a few drinks, then crash out.

Day Three was the longest: 184 miles from Kinsale to the Aran Islands, rounding Ireland's barren and awesome south-west coast. It took us through the treacherous channel at the Blaskets, and out into the big Atlantic seas.

There was no let-up from the moment we left Kinsale; we all kept going for ten long hours, stopping only for the occasional snack. Visibility was poor as we aimed for headland after headland appearing out of the gloom. Through the fog we got barely a glimpse of the Fastnet Rock off our port side as we drove inside it. And travelling inside the Skelligs we all tended to slow down when anyone began to drift behind, for fear we should lose sight of them. After Dingle we were out into the big rollers and massive swell of the Atlantic Ocean.

[*Alan Priddy commented later:* We hit a whale. We just came across the top of a big wave, and it was there in the trough; as we came down, the boat landed on it and stopped dead. The whale submerged, and we were all ejected from our seats — two in the front of the boat, one whose nose was splattered all over the console. It was just one of those things. It was the bow that hit it. It must have had a bruise, but they're big animals. It was probably a whale or possibly a large basking shark; they grow up to 35 feet, but they're completely harmless as they are filter feeders.]

It was a good, if boisterous, evening in the pub on Inishmore that evening, and the next morning we nursed a hangover or two as we headed to Rossaveal Quay on the mainland to refuel.

Unfortunately, with so many bays on the coast, it was difficult to distinguish the entrance of Cashla Bay which leads to Rossaveal, and we totted up 20 miles trying to find it.

Once we were refuelled, the rest of Day Four, heading for Killybegs in brilliant sunshine, was the most exhilarating passage of the trip. The rollers were so gigantic that it was like driving up a steep hill at 30 knots. At the top, there would be a lingering moment where you seemed to stop and could take in the views of the magnificent coast, the trawlers and the thousands of puffins and other sea birds in the air and resting in great flocks on the surface of the rolling sea, before dropping over the other side like tumbling down a roller coaster ride.

There was a tremendous reception for us at the busy fishing port of Killybegs, where many of the locals had turned out to watch us arrive.

For the home run to Bangor, on Day Five, I travelled with Jan Falkowski, a psychiatrist from London, in *The Shrink*, his Ribtec 645 powered by a single 150hp Mariner outboard. The weather was at its most clement and, though the sea was quite flat for most of the day, we were dogged all along that north coast stretch by miles of drift nets with green floats that were tricky to see in the water. The journey became excruciatingly slow and we decided the best way to make progress was to just motor up fairly fast, kill the engine, lift up the leg and glide over them: fine, as long as you could see where they were. Jean-Pierre cut the top of a net doing this, but managed to get through.

The Shrink, though, got caught up badly on a net and one of the crew had to jump into the water to cut the line. There was a fear he might get caught in the net and be dragged under by the current — fortunately, he didn't, but he did cut his hand badly on the monofilament line.

Under way on *The Shrink*, we had a survival-packed lunch of cold lamb stew with carrots, followed by liquidised apricot and plum dessert. Imagine, if you can, trying to swig jam at 35 knots.

As we happened to be passing, we all joined Garth's boat in taking the opportunity to stop off at their home town of Portrush, halfway between Killybegs and Bangor, to meet up with friends, share a drink and tell some tales.

Entering Bangor there was an odd but satisfying feeling to be coming back to the point where we had started, and of course a tremendous sense of achievement. Yet for all that, it was a bit of an anticlimax, mainly because there was no one there to meet us.

On paper, the journey was predicted as 750 miles but, what with going in and out of harbours, and up and down waves, we made 940 miles. The convoy did, however, manage it in a record elapsed sea time for a circumnavigation of Ireland, of 44 hours, 11 minutes and 50 seconds.

We had a bit of a party that night and presented ourselves with medals for being so clever — because not only had we fulfilled an ambition and broken a record, but our adventure raised £2000 for multiple sclerosis research, thanks to sponsorship by various commercial and marine companies, and from fund raising throughout the event by the Rotary Club of Southsea Castle. We felt very grateful for the enthusiastic support shown to us, and generosity towards the event, from all the people we met at every stop.

It was sad to split up the next morning. The three RIBs who had crossed from Conwy made their way back together. A couple mentioned stopping off at the Isle of Man for a RIB event that was taking place there. Before departing, there was talk of getting together for another adventure — perhaps the Bay of Biscay, or to St Petersburg. The words "glutton" and "punishment" crossed my mind, but only briefly — by now I understood the thrill.

For the coming RIB racing season, I hope to muster an MBY team: I just need to persuade a couple of other members of staff to join me. I'll pitch it simply: "Look, it's not all salt water blisters, rough sea and exhaustion. Well, OK, yes it is. But that can be fun. Honest."

Many thanks to Denis O'Neill and IPC for this article.

FOUR : 1996 : ACROSS BISCAY

After three gruelling trips in previous years it was a pleasant change to cruise in 1994 and 1995, but for Alan Priddy there was always the itch to try something else. He cannot really remember when it was he had the idea of trying to cross the Atlantic in a RIB, but feels sure it must have been during one of those trips that are what 'ribbing' is all about — calm seas, heavenly sunshine, good company … Anyway, the seed was sown and he started to put the plan into action for crossing the Atlantic in 1997 by the "over the top" route as early as January 1996.

The plan was simple — ship the boat over to Portsmouth, New Hampshire and follow the coast along to Nova Scotia and Labrador, before crossing up to Greenland and then down to Iceland and home. An evening's work on the world-wide planner soon highlighted the long sea passages that he would have to undertake in order to fulfil the ambition; the longest leg would be 750 nautical miles.

At that time it was important to demonstrate to potential sponsors and helpers that they were not completely mad, and the by then established crew of Alan, Jan, Steve and Vic agreed that a trip of similar distance should be undertaken to prove it could be done. They discounted the idea of a large circular trip, such as the Scillies, the Channel Islands and back, as too easy — if they developed a problem, help would be too readily to hand — so they decided to cross the Bay of Biscay from Bilbao to Portsmouth non-stop, a distance of 610 nm.

The winter months came and went, and before they knew it the time had come to load *Still Never Enough* on to *The Pride of Bilbao* for its 36 hour crossing to Spain. They took the time on the ferry to relax and go through the logistics of fuel and equipment. They knew it was going to be a journey of not less than 610 miles, but had to allow for 20% extra fuel to account for the "going up and down" syndrome — in big seas you may travel forward 30 feet, but if you have to drive up a 20-foot wave and down the other side, you have used 70 feet worth of fuel. They knew the boat used fuel at a rate of 1 litre every 1.25 nautical miles, so they had loaded 650 litres of fuel in England — enough for 800 miles, the 'worst-case' scenario…

Somehow it became a race — no one is sure how — between the ferry and the RIB. It seemed a good time to aim for, and would be a good guide for the Atlantic legs if they could get to Portsmouth before the *Pride of Bilbao*.

On June 12, 1996 the boat and crew arrived in Spain and immediately prepared the boat for disembarkation. They had made arrangements beforehand to be met by members of the Rotary Club of

Bilbao, and their brief was to arrange removal to the nearest slipway so they could launch the boat and make the best of the daylight hours. There was just one problem — the tide was out. In order to get away on time something had to be done urgently, so Jan disappeared with one of the Spaniards while the other three gave interviews to all the Spanish press. Their reaction was that the crew were crazy, and Alan realised afterwards that the coverage was good because the media were convinced the little boat and its crew would never be seen again.

Jan appeared with a police escort. No one asked how, but he had convinced the port manager to lend one of the large container cranes to launch the boat, and the police were there to provide an escort back into the dock to where they could launch. As with all Mediterranean countries a certain amount of convincing was necessary, and soon every Spaniard in the vicinity sported a Musto hat; even the crew ended up hatless. But the boat was launched and they were ready.

The weather forecast was not as good as it could have been — north-westerly, force 4 or 5, straight on the nose — so they knew they were in for a rough time. Setting off at 1000, the first 100 miles were covered in 3.5 hours, and then, as if by the flick of a switch, the wind started to blow. In an instant huge rolling seas with breaking tops were coming down on the boat from all directions.

Down to 19 knots and shipping water continuously, the crew began to have doubts over the next 25 miles as to the wisdom of continuing. Alan regretted not fitting a self-righting system, convinced the boat was going to go over. But it didn't, a true testimony to the excellent sea-keeping of a RIB.

At the 125 mile mark the engine died. Shortage of fuel was suspected, but under normal conditions, they should have returned 150 miles from the main tank, and a refuelling stop wasn't due for another hour. They refuelled the main tank, bled the system of all air, and turned the key. Nothing. It felt as if the battery was flat, so it was back into the engine box with huge amounts of diesel rolling around the bilges, and seas breaking over the side of the boat. With hindsight, someone remembered the sea anchor, but it was too late — sea sickness had set in and Alan was feeling the worse for wear. The key was turned once more; whatever he had done had worked, and the engine fired into life. Pausing only briefly to lean over the side, they were under way, Alan recalling a conversation with Chris Kaye about how the latter had come back from an abortive trip to Iceland on his wing engine. He had been lucky — the Biscay crew had a wing engine, too, but because it was petrol and they only had enough fuel for 20 miles, it would not be of much help when they were 150 miles from the nearest land...

Alan prides himself on maintaining his boat to a fault, so when the engine started to surge on its own at the 150 mile mark, he felt sick inside. It was soon established that one of the main wires in the wiring loom had broken through, a very easy job to fix. The problem was that the engine had to be stopped to do it. A discussion between the crew took place — if we turn the engine off, will it start again? They couldn't be sure the starter motor or battery were in good enough working order and would be able to restart the engine after the repair. Jan came up with the good idea that now would be a good time to start rationing food and drink because they might be faced with drifting towards Portugal for the next four days before help was at hand. Jan knows how to say the right thing at the right time...

With the engine turned off and the offending wire repaired, they decided to "hot-wire" the engine so when (and if) it did start, the only way to stop it would be to run it out of fuel. The key was turned, and it started. They were under way again. Only 460 miles to go.

The next 150 miles were quite awful, with huge breaking head seas slowing them down, and it was dark as they approached Ushant with only the hand-held GPS left working — and using batteries up at an alarming rate — and they were reduced to going round in circles until daybreak so they could make out a landmark so as not to end up on the rocks. Daybreak came at about 0330 and, safely through Ushant, a well-earned rest was called for. The flask of hot water was brought out, and the first hot drink for 20 hours passed sunburnt and sore lips. Some 12 hours behind schedule, with no chance of making it up, the head seas continued their battering, and a tactical decision was made to run the boat in the best direction north as they could to maintain 20 knots. After 30 minutes of this they checked the charts and estimated that their landfall might be Weymouth before they would get the shelter of the land for the run home.

They sighted the shores of England after 31 hours at sea, running low on fuel because of the big seas and the amended route, so a quick trip into Weymouth for a top-up was agreed on. As it turned out, they did have enough fuel for the rest of the trip, but with 650 nm already logged, erred on the side of caution.

Telephone contact was made with anxious families, and it was a few minutes before 7 pm that they tied up outside the Bridge Tavern in Old Portsmouth. It had taken 34 hours, and they had logged 710 nautical miles, using 600 litres of fuel.

But they had proved that a small boat could do what would be classed as an open sea voyage. The Big One was possible.

Some important lessons had been learned. Alan made a list:

[1] You can never have enough fuel; you should always over-estimate.

[2] The boat must have two seats you can sleep in. Two high backed bucket seats with harnesses would be fitted so two crew could relax (unless rough, when harnesses would not be used).

[3] Crew should rotate jobs at least every 100 miles to prevent boredom.

[4] The sea anchor should be deployed if stopping, to avoid broaching.

[5] There should be a canopy over the engine, so you can work on it without the engine box filling with water.

[6] Along with a spare battery, there should be a small generator to charge the batteries. It was no good repairing the engine if the battery was too flat to start it!

It hardly needs to be said that such modifications are with the trans-Atlantic trip in mind. Alan was keen not to create the impression that everyone going out in a RIB needs to take such severe measures. However, they are not without a little common sense.

They did not quite beat the ferry; but then, Alan reasoned, the trans-Atlantic crossing would not be a race. They had proved themselves, and the crew looked little the worse for wear; in addition, they had nothing but praise for their Musto HPX Drysuits and for the boat itself.

The press were most impressed with the Biscay achievement, and Alan could feel a certain amount of media momentum picking up for the major adventure to come.

It is at this point, with the knowledge that legs of 600 miles plus could be achieved, and if necessary in bad weather, that the Atlantic Challenge looks possible. But many things are possible; it doesn't mean they have to be attempted, or that they are going to be successful. To those of us who know very little about the sea, and even those who know a lot about the sea, it still rather begs the question: "Why?"

FIVE : ATLANTIC CHALLENGE

Why <u>would</u> anyone want to cross the Atlantic in an open boat, particularly the north bit of it, when you can cross it in about 4 hours by Concorde, 8 by Jumbo, or — if you must go by sea — in a few days in supreme comfort on an ocean liner? Certainly not to get to the other side.

Eric the Red (who lived from about AD940-1010) did part of it, in about the year 982, when he sailed to Greenland and founded a colony there. But the other circumstances worth mentioning are that, first, <u>his</u> open boat was the latest and fastest form of transport available at the time and, second (and perhaps more important) Eric just happened to have been banished from Iceland for murder. Going back to Norway was not an option (guess why), and so he struck out westwards. How many ships were lost on the way, no one knows, and the Vikings themselves did not seem to be particularly bothered; apparently, from one fleet of 24 ships crossing from Iceland to Greenland, 10 were recorded as lost without further comment. It may not seem far across the Denmark Strait on the map, but you will see later that this is at the opposite end of 'plain sailing', especially when you remember that Eric would have had to sail out of sight of land for many days — without a compass.

Leif Ericsson, Eric the Red's son is, according to tradition, the first Euro-Scandinavian to have sailed from Greenland to what we now know as North America, completing his father's journey across the Atlantic probably in about the year 997. He stayed for a winter, confirmed by a Norwegian expedition in 1963 which found traces of his settlement in what he called 'Vinland', and presumably returned to Greenland, where American indian arrowheads have been found by other archeologists.

The Vikings settled in Britain, of course (among their descendants was William "the Conqueror"), and their blood, though a little dilute by now, will still run in the veins of many inhabitants of the British Isles and consequently North America. Perhaps not so diluted in Alan Priddy's case. But as well as their blood, and perhaps because Britain has remained an island, the sea is never far away from our eyes and our thoughts. The Viking heritage has always been heroic adventure, and more mundanely the source of some seafaring terms including the word 'starboard', from the steer-board which was always on the right of the stern.

There is no reason, just because we don't have historical records, to suppose that no one else crossed the Atlantic after Eric's time and before the 'official' discovery by rich and royally-sponsored explorers several hundred years later. It is possible that people from Iceland fished as far out as Greenland, or even in the rich fishing grounds off Nova Scotia. We will probably never know.

It's fortunate, then that stability and wealth in Europe in the 15th century enabled people like Jean (John) Cabot to make their mark on world history. Cabot (1450-1498) was an Italian navigator, who made many voyages to the Levant (the eastern Mediterranean). In 1484 he moved to London. Commissioned with his 3 sons by Henry VII to 'discover unknown lands', he arrived at Cape Breton Island on 24 June, 1497 thus, according to tradition, discovering the North American mainland (the fact that <u>he</u> thought he was in north east Asia can be ignored). He apparently sailed again the following year, and touched Greenland, and probably died on the voyage.

Cabot's ship, *Matthew,* although probably one of the most advanced ships of its day, could not sail into the wind, so the journey would have been difficult. No log of Cabot's voyage has been found, and we only know that he was given a letter patent from Henry VII, giving him the right to fly the English banner while he sailed to discover new lands — not so dissimilar from the mission statement heard at the start of every episode of Star Trek. While there was no log, though, Peter Snow did disclose in the BBC series "The Voyage of the *Matthew*" that, in a castle in Spain in 1955, a researcher found a letter written to Columbus by an English spy, John Day, giving some details of Cabot's voyage, such as crew, duration, course, and what happened when *Matthew* got to America.

It is hard to imagine the deprivations suffered at sea several centuries ago without any of today's modern conveniences, but then in several centuries' time, people will wonder at Alan Priddy's achievement with today's 'primitive' technology. It is all relative. There were two significant differences between Cabot's crew and Alan Priddy's. The first was in dietary requirements — sailors on *Matthew* would have drunk a gallon of beer a day and consumed 6000 calories of food each, whereas Alan's calorie requirements were 1600 a day with no beer (none admitted, anyway). The other difference is that Henry VII gave Cabot £10 for founding what is now Canada, whereas Alan was unable to find a royal sponsor — unfortunately, the whole world has been discovered. There are people who could sponsor the modern equivalent of Cabot's voyage — a journey into space — but there appear to be no takers.

Sebastian Cabot (1474-1557), the second son of John, was also an explorer, and navigator and cartographer. He was employed by royalty, too, including Henry VIII.

I suppose we must mention Columbus, who discovered the West Indies in 1492, but did not sight the American mainland until 1498 — about a year after Cabot.

In all these voyages of discovery, there is one significant link; they were all from east to west. Alan Priddy is going to do it the other way. He is going to do it, in those famous words of John F Kennedy: "...not because it is easy, but because it is hard." Each thing Alan does has to be harder than the one before. Otherwise, he cannot be satisfied. One wonders where it will end — if he could drive the RIB to the moon, he would probably consider that, too.

If all this serves only to confuse rather than enlighten as to why Alan and his crew want to cross the Atlantic in an open boat, it is not surprising. It is notoriously difficult to analyse why people do unusual things, and perhaps one should not try too hard. No one asked Scott why he still went to the pole when he almost certainly knew Amundsen had by far the better chance of getting there first. People intent on standing on top of a mountain have been asked why, too, and a classic reply is "because it's there." It is a romantic notion, but there are other reasons.

Perhaps we should look at some of those other reasons in Alan Priddy's case. Those astute enough to notice that 1997 is the 1000th anniversary (or thereabouts) of Leif Ericsson's crossing to North America from Greenland and the 500th anniversary of John Cabot's crossing of the Atlantic to Cape Breton will already have seen one reason.

Another is that Alan has a link with North America through his sister and her husband, who live in Maine. Portsmouth, New Hampshire is popular with north eastern Americans, and is high on their list of first class leisure centres. It was natural that Alan, coming from Portsmouth in England, should want to start his crossing from its namesake city.

Important, too, is Alan's keenness to visit new places and meet new people before — he says — he is too old. Oh yes, and he wouldn't mind being famous. Driving an open boat through areas where an icebreaker is usually the minimum requirement is one certain way of attracting attention, and there must be something of the attention seeker in all explorers. But who can object to a desire to be famous if they are prepared to go to such lengths?

Another indispensable ingredient is Alan's love of, and flair for organising. The scale of the Atlantic operation would daunt the most accomplished project manager in a multi-national company. But just how complex is a venture of this nature? Well, first you have to have the idea.

The idea

Alan first had the idea (he thinks) to cross the Atlantic while on his way to the London Boat Show in January 1996, and it was brought about by not knowing what to do next. He had done Round Britain,

Round Ireland and gone as far south as Spain, so when he arrived at the show and people kept asking what he was going to do next, the Atlantic seemed like a fitting sequel. He sat down with his friends and a computer and worked out that at least in theory it was achievable to drive a RIB from Portsmouth USA to Portsmouth UK and a tentative date was agreed for June/July 1997.

So early in the year, a simple plan was envisaged: to retrace (in the opposite direction) the route of the great explorer John Cabot, who on 23 June 1497 first sighted Cape Breton after his crossing from the UK, and to sight the same landfall 500 years later, to the day. A simple enough mission statement.

For Alan, the trip will be the adventure of a lifetime. It is the Greenland leg which holds the most excitement, though in theory they will have the option of missing Greenland if they want to, from the fuel point of view. But, as Alan often says, the secret of success is meticulous planning; he likes to know that every small detail is covered before he leaves.

There are a million things to be done. Not least of Alan's concerns is the length of each sea leg, but the Biscay trip has at least answered that question. Next are a thousand questions about the conditions they will encounter, the places they will need to refuel and the equipment they will need to take. Not least on a list of supplementary questions is — will they be fit enough? It is worth expanding on some of the items on Alan's growing list as 1996 unfolds.

Clothing

Dry suits will be essential, and the Musto clothing proved itself to the crew during their run across the Bay of Biscay. Some suits can be quite restricting, but these are not; looking at them, with the zip across the back of the shoulders, they look uncomfortable, but certainly are not. All their previous suits have had zips at the front, but a zip is a potential leakage area, whereas if it's across the back, and up high, and you're in the water, the possibility for leakage is minimised. Alan also makes a note to have the suits altered to have a six inch fly zip put in; the problem with some suits is if you have to take the suit off to have a pee, and it is pouring with rain, you're going to be soaked by the time you put it back on.

Communications

Besides communicating about conditions, the crew will need to keep in touch with home, weather organisations, the media and stopovers.

At all times they will need to know where they are (it sounds obvious), and how far they are from their destination. None of this can be done without modern technology, and access to satellite information.

Conditions

It may be stating the obvious to say that conditions at sea are determined solely by the weather. Time (unless you are running out of fuel) means little, and dates mean less. Traffic is irrelevant. That there will be ice is in no doubt. On the route envisaged, taking in Greenland, there is always ice. How much ice, where it will be and, perhaps most important, where it is going, will not be known for certain until the day before. The study of ice, Alan knows, could be a lifetime's work, and therefore to the sailor it comes down to trusting the experts.

Weather forecasts will be crucial. But if British weather forecasters cannot see a hurricane coming, will their Arctic counterparts be any more proficient? These are questions which cannot yet be answered, because the weather in 1997, as in all other years, will be unique. And such is the complexity of the weather patterns in the North Atlantic that some observers have been heard to say a guess is as good a forecast as any.

What is certain is that conditions will be tough. From summer temperatures in New Hampshire, there could be 50°C difference in Greenland. They have to be sure the boat, the engine, the equipment and the crew are prepared for all eventualities.

Crew

There is no question about who the crew is. Alan, Jan, Steve and Vic are a team. There is no question of reserves. Already, this team hold the record for driving a RIB round Britain, Ireland and Scotland, and it would be nonsense to introduce someone new at this stage. Alan is quite adamant — if anyone drops out, their seat will be taken out of the boat. The trip could be done with three; only two people are actually needed to control the boat — one watching and one driving — while the other sleeps.

Finances

Alan has estimated the trip will cost in the region of £65,000, a great deal of which will be his own money. The rest will be raised from sponsors, either in cash or in kind. Alan is good at raising money, and his record helps. Many sponsors on this trip are loyal supporters from the past. The media coverage already generated helps, too. Confirmed press and TV coverage is the best encouragement for potential sponsors.

It doesn't, though finish when the boat is brought ashore at the end of the trip, because there will be more money to be spent on return.

Fitness

Early in 1996, an uneasy feeling is hovering in Alan's mind — are we fit enough? All right, it's not going to be a race, just fast cruising, and the object is to get home safely. The plan will be to drive for an hour or two, then rest for twenty minutes. In bad weather, being bounced up and down continuously means you need regular relief, for the limbs, the kidneys, and the concentration. Resting does not necessarily mean stopping; reducing speed to 6 or 7 knots, the boat becomes a stable platform to move about on or perhaps cook, even in the middle of the ocean. This team probably have more experience in this kind of boating than any other in the world, and they will be able to apply the lessons they've learned.

But that is not to say there will not be side effects. Tiredness will come quickly, especially in the cold weather. Seasickness may affect them. The strain of just staying in the boat will take its toll; toe straps help, but the knees, thighs, backs and arms take a great deal of punishment, even when sitting or lying down. For Alan, the answer is simple. Ask the experts. He will be seeking the advice of Portsmouth University Fitness Department.

Fuel

The boat will have a maximum range of 1200 miles, and it will be possible to achieve this incredible potential by fitting extra fuel tanks on the deck. Comfort breaks will also allow the opportunity to transfer fuel, electrically or manually, from the auxiliary tanks into the main fuel tank, so the engine never has to be shut down. In the Arctic, there will be few places to fill up.

Media

When considering media coverage, it helps to have a reputation. The Biscay adventure helped considerably, but simply announcing a new and daring challenge does not mean automatic coverage. Many sporting challenges are announced each year, and most are largely ignored by the media — they know that most do not survive even the first setback.

The difference in media reaction in the case of Alan Priddy is simple to explain — credentials. Alan and his crew are probably the most experienced team to undertake this difficult and demanding style of boating. In many respects they are trail blazers, not only in the field of trans-Atlantic navigation, but in terms of taking to sea in a standard style of boat with an exceptional safety record and a seagoing performance which combines speed with sea-kindly behaviour. And because the appeal of RIBs extends beyond intrepid navigators typified by Alan, to family sailors who just wish to cruise along Britain's coasts or across the narrow seas to France, Belgium and Holland, interest will be massive. Put all this together with the good humour exhibited by the crew, and Alan's ability to handle interviews so well, and the magic formula is there. One powerboating journalist was heard to comment that sailors were ten a penny and all that 'sticks and strings' stuff cut no ice with his readers — a nice simple thing like a motor boat that can cross the Atlantic, a mere 24 feet long with a diesel engine — was something they could relate to.

Regular coverage in the regional press and specialist publications helps, of course, and Alan has featured many times in these, but it requires a special effort to interest the national media, and that is where Alan is pleased to have enlisted the help of Brian Pilcher. When coverage of the event is confirmed for the London International Boat Show programme, which will be screened by the BBC in January 1997, it will be a step in the right direction. Regional TV is showing an interest, too. The ideal coverage, of course, a 2 or 3 part mini series covering the preparation and the voyage itself with onboard footage is already under discussion.

Interest is strong in the USA, too, where the challenge has captured the imagination, perhaps even more so than in the UK.

Alan is already considering film rights. Unfortunately, he is hampered by the fact that bad news is the best news. If they die in the attempt, every film company in the world will be bidding. That's life, if you'll forgive the pun.

Navigation

On board, in the open sea, on a deck only a few feet above the water, radar may not be very effective. It will be light, continuously in the high latitudes, but visibility could be poor owing to fog, rain or big seas. At the speeds the boat will be travelling, tides will have little effect, but unfavourable winds could make sea-going difficult. GPS will be constantly in use, backed up by charts, rather than the other way around. Alan is hopeful of testing out some of Magellan's latest technology.

Personal affairs

It is easy to forget that this is not just a short break from work, a strenuous holiday. Things could go wrong — they could be iced up in Greenland for a month. It is best to be prepared for everything — even injury or fatality. And just as important during the hectic year's planning for the event is to relieve the burden in other areas. So one of the things Alan has had unfortunately to jettison is his place on the committee of BIBOA (British Inflatable Boat Owners Association).

There is also the aftermath to be considered. For a few weeks after the event, interest will be high until, in the natural order of things, the public — and the media — turn their attention to other events. So Alan has allowed for that, and acknowledged that afterwards he will need a holiday. He has rented a cottage so he and his family can take a quiet break in Dartmouth for three weeks. With the boat, of course.

Record Books

An excellent means of attracting media attention — and fame — is to achieve an entry in the Guinness Book of Records. Negotiations are already under way to secure this. Discussions first have to take place with the ruling body of boating sports, The Royal Yachting Association, who have approved an outline plan for recording the total passage time for the trans-Atlantic voyage from Portsmouth, USA to Portsmouth, UK. The United States Coastguard will officiate at the start and the Royal Albert Yacht Club and Royal Naval Club will set up a finish line between Spitsand Fort and Southsea Castle. The firing of a cannon will salute the return of Alan Priddy and his crew to home waters and signal the end of their crossing.

Intermediate leg times will be authenticated by harbour authority officials in stopovers such as Labrador and Greenland where the sport of yachting has not yet led to the formation of recognised yacht clubs.

Breaking a new route means that the crew is setting target times for subsequent adventurers following the same course. Until that happens, Alan Priddy and his companions can expect to be the only seafarers to have undertaken such an adventurous, high latitude voyage across one of the world's most feared oceans, west to east.

Route

The route is decided early in 1996. It will be Portsmouth, New Hampshire to Portsmouth, Hampshire via Nova Scotia, Belle Isle Strait to

Battle Harbour, Nanortalik in Greenland, Reykjavik in Iceland and Bangor, Northern Ireland. Given that the boat can travel 1200 miles without refuelling, there is the option, if ice is bad, to miss Greenland altogether. During the summer, some of the Arctic ice breaks up and drifts southwards, and it is difficult to predict from year to year which harbours will be open at particular times.

Safety

Uppermost in Alan's mind is the possibility of mishap. The RIB is supremely stable, and has never turned over, even in the roughest seas, although it came close to it once, Alan admits. If it does turn over, it will float upside down, and there are ways of getting it upright by letting some of the tubes down and then re-inflating them again by foot pump. This is not to be recommended, however, in water which may be close to freezing point and home to some of the world's most efficient carnivores, including polar bears or even sharks.

Medical requisites have to be thoroughly thought out; if an injury occurs, help could be hours or even days away. Alan is reliant on Dr Jan Falkowski for this part of the project, but he even has to consider what would happen if Jan himself were injured, so the principle is to make it as certain as possible that the potential for injury of any kind is minimised. That includes ensuring secure stowage, safe sleeping arrangements and even considering fire risk.

Sponsors and Suppliers

Alan and his crew will disembark at the Bridge Tavern in Old Portsmouth at the end of their journey. There is some evidence that this area was the very first place in England that potatoes were landed by Christopher Columbus. Alan has therefore asked Gales Ales, the owners of the tavern, if they would consider producing a commemorative beer. He will also be asking a brewer in Portsmouth, New Hampshire, if they will do the same.

They will be using an identical power unit in the boat for the Atlantic Challenge to that which powered them across the Bay of Biscay, only it will be brand new. Yamaha will consequently be one of the sponsors. Many people outside the boating world do not realise that Yamaha make diesel engines — since they are one of the most successful companies in the world, they don't feel the need to promote the fact heavily.

Among other sponsors already lined up will be Ribtec, the

builders of the Alan's RIB. The list of sponsors will grow as the year progresses.

Start and Finish

Among the million things to do are two of the most important — the start and the finish. Alan has been well-received in Portsmouth, New Hampshire; his home town of Portsmouth, England, has made him their 51st Envoy, a great honour (Alan's enquiry about the diplomatic plates and cheque card were perhaps a little optimistic), and when he walked unannounced into City Hall (NH) the Mayor, Eileen Foley, was there to greet him within a minute or two. She quickly introduced Alan to her director of economic planning, Mark Kellerer. The start of the challenge is expected to be a great day for Portsmouth, New Hampshire. Although a popular resort, it is a relatively quiet city much of the time.

The day the boat arrives back in the UK will be the first day of the Disabled Olympics, but Alan is assured that it will not diminish his achievement. Many people will recall that when Alec Rose came home, thousands came to see him.

Two questions about the finish sprang to Alan's mind early in the planning stages — what if he's late, and what if he's early? His answer to the former is characteristic — he won't be. His view is that if he is that late, something serious will have happened, and the event will have already been abandoned. As to the other question, he plans to take a week to come from Ireland to Portsmouth, so there is time to 'wind up' the media and put the name of Portsmouth firmly on the world map. The last overnight stop will be Weymouth, and Alan plans to be there on the Thursday. He will arrange for the boat to be hidden round the back of the harbour, arriving late at night and keeping a low profile to draw the media into speculation.

Supporters

As with all Alan's trips, he and the crew always raise money for charity, and it has usually been left to Alan to decide on a worthy cause, but for this trip, Steve Lloyd suggested the Cancer Care Society, where he had recently fitted a carpet in their Centre in Romsey and realised their need for urgent funds. The crew all believe in putting something back into society if you have the chance. Without blowing their own trumpets, they have raised a considerable amount of money between them, not only as a boating team, but with the Rotary Club as well.

The Cancer Care Society are a low profile organisation, started in the 1970s, and have become an island of hope for the victims of cancer and their families and friends through counselling and psychological support. They help in other ways, too, including the provision of wigs, desperately needed in cases of hair loss as a result of treatment. The Society's earnest wish is to open more centres and be able to help more people, and Steve was impressed by their sincerity and quiet, hard work. When Alan approached them with his offer, they were overwhelmed, if a little in awe of what he was doing. Kim Fielder of the CCS, and Lord and Lady Romsey will be closely involved in supporting the challenge.

Not least of Alan's concerns about involving the community is the opportunity to involve schools in the challenge. He is approaching several on both sides of the Atlantic, and will announce his intention of trying to set up satellite data links so their pupils can follow his progress day by day.

A fixed idea

Eventually, then, as these and many other threads begin to weave themselves into a coherent whole, the Atlantic Challenge is becoming a reality. By October 1996, much of what is termed in modern business-speak, infrastructure, is in place. Accompanied by Vic Palmer on a whistle-stop tour of Maine and New Hampshire, Alan is fêted by the Portsmouth, NH, Rotary Club, who achieve a massive turnout of over 70% of members at a luncheon held in his honour. In his brief address to the members, Alan outlines the project and tells them that he has been appointed as an Envoy of Portsmouth City Council in Hampshire to assist in the promotion of business and tourist links between the communities of the two cities, a sentiment warmly greeted by those present. The visit is a complete success with all the necessary arrangements being made for the pre-start preparation period and the departure, which will be organised and timed by the US Coastguard.

Portsmouth, New Hampshire shares many features with its elder sister in the UK: both have important naval dockyards and fortifications at the water's edge which have seen action over hundreds of years — there is even a Sally Port in the fortifications of both cities. Alan is almost overwhelmed by the warmth of his reception and the cooperation over the trip. All the civic leaders from the Mayor, Eileen Foley, to the Police Chief and Senior Coastguard are quite clearly on his side. They expect several public events to be staged at Strawberry Banke, an open air museum facing on to the Piscataqua River, where the boat will be on display before departure. Alan is keen to bring the two cities closer together as they have much to offer each other.

During his visit, Alan has finalised the dates for the voyage. He has met with the US Coastguard and other organisations who might have been in a position to stop him leaving; because of the regulations on small boat movements, it is necessary to get permission from the head office of the Coastguard in Boston. There are meetings with the British Consulate for their approval, and also with all the media in a 250 mile radius.

By November 1996, the last components of the plans are slotting into place. The boat will be delivered to Alan's sister's house in Maine (a reassuring element of homeliness in this international event), some 60 miles north of Portsmouth, for safe keeping some time in late April (1997). Vic and Alan will arrive one week before the June 22 start to recommission the boat, as it will be in a stripped down state when it arrives in the USA. The boat will then be taken by trailer to Wentworth by the Sea's Marina just south of Portsmouth for most of the public relations work.

On Saturday, 21 June the boat will be moved to Prescott Park in the centre of Portsmouth, NH, where a weekend festival is being organised by the city. There will be a live band, side stalls and a chance for the public to see the boat and meet the crew.

On Sunday, 22 June after a short blessing they will make their way out of Portsmouth Harbour escorted by the Coastguard to Sally Point, the entrance to the harbour. At 1 pm a gun will be fired and they will be on their way to Nova Scotia some 650 miles away.

And as if the plans are not complex enough, actually putting them into practice is another matter entirely. But before the curtain rises on the dramas of Summer, 1997, we need to meet the players.

SIX : THE CREW — THE RIGHT STUFF

To do something that hasn't been done before — voluntarily — takes a person of a certain calibre. Whether it's a mountain, a pothole, a jungle, a dive or a sea voyage doesn't matter. It's the common denominator — that step out into the void — that matters. Most of us can't do that. We cling to what we know and read about the rest in books like this one. There's nothing wrong with that — we can't all be going out on adventures every day. But one thing such an exploit does do, and that is it injects into each of us just a tiny bit of uneasiness about our safe and predictable existence so tomorrow — or maybe next week — we might go and do something just a little bit unconventional and adventurous. And that tendency has to be good for each of us, and for society.

Of course there can only ever be a handful of Priddys at a time, wanting to be adventurous all the time, but heaven help us if one day there are none.

To get some idea of what sort of people are going to set out on this modern day epic, here are just a few facts and quotes. Just a few — there cannot be any better way of getting to know four adventurers than by reading of their adventures, and you've read some of those already.

Alan Priddy

Alan was born in Portsmouth in 1953, the son of a Portsmouth aircraft builder, and was apprenticed as a boat builder. It's partly the fact that he has been the MD of an engineering company for 26 years now that drives him to do silly things in small boats. He has been married three times and has two teenaged sons and step-daughter. James, his elder son, will be making an important contribution to the Atlantic Challenge.

Alan was only ten when he built his first canoe out of an old deck chair and launched it in the stream running past his home in Havant, part of Bedhampton Creek. The canoe was modelled on those used by World War II commandos, the Cockleshell Heroes, and their exploits fired Alan's imagination. During the summer, the water level would fall, and he would dam the stream so he could boat all year round. In the ensuing years, he developed a love of the sea, learned to sail and owned most types of boat before catching the RIB bug in 1989.

A sailor, navigator and RIB driver of many years' standing now, nobody knows better the hazards — and pleasures — of putting to sea in a well prepared, fast craft. He doesn't use his boat as much as he used to, but he goes further — on a 200 or 400 mile journey, such as to the Scillies or Belgium, or the West Country.   In a typical year, he can log as much as 6000 miles, because he uses the boat much as others would use a family car. His partner, Liz, accepts the boating as part of their life, though would be quite happy on four wheels.

Already a member of Sparkes Cruising Club on Hayling Island, Alan has become a member of the Royal Dorset Yacht Club, and gave them a talk in November 1997. His idea is to encourage not only RIB owners, but all small boat owners, to be more adventurous. He feels it is a shame that the boating industry is so short-sighted they cannot see that the advantage of promoting small boats is far better than building big boats — they can build small boats so much quicker, so much more cost effectively. There's a trend to go from big boats to small ones, anyway, because people are more likely to use a small boat every weekend, whereas a big boat, with the extra effort required, is used less often.

Alan is a founder member of the Southsea Castle Rotary Club and a member of RIBex, the first organisation for rigid inflatable owners (principally an eating and drinking club that you tend to go to by RIB) which organises occasional expeditions by RIB, finishing near a hostelry.

Jan Falkowski

At 36 years of age, Jan is the youngest of the crew, and is London-based. He is a doctor with some military training and is a veteran of all the long-distance trips. His parents come from Poland, and his father is a psychiatrist, so it is not surprising Jan chose to become a consultant in the same branch of medicine.

Jan is divorced, and has two children and two rottweilers; his girlfriend, Jane Hodge, lives in Farlington. Jane is of course concerned, but like all the spouses of the crew, has accepted that they are determined to undertake the challenge across the Atlantic. Jan still has *The Shrink*; he has been 'doing things' on the water for about 10 years.

He doesn't smile readily, and those who don't know him might think he was a worrier. But the only thing he confesses to worrying about is not being able to do the trip because of ice.

Although nominally second skipper, it is Jan's principal job on board *Spirit of Portsmouth* to look for the first signs of illness or stress among the crew. He is aware the cold will cause dehydration and disorientation which could affect decision-making, so he will be ensuring the crew keep up their fluid intake. Despite the fact that he will be subjected to the same stresses as the others, he will nevertheless have to watch out for the classic signs of problems among the crew; the effects of continuous high speed cruising are varied, and include disruption of eating habits and body rhythms. Tiredness itself is not a helpful clue, since normal daily routine will be disrupted anyway. In short, it is Jan's job to see that the crew survive — even in the best conditions, there is the chance of injury, or a breakdown beyond the reach of immediate help.

The medical supplies will include the full military trauma pack which will contain morphine and other necessities in case of injury. Common painkillers for minor injuries will probably not be taken for fear of masking pain and worsening the injury. There is also a good supply of seasickness tablets, which can be taken prior to working on the engine, for example, or simply to make it easier to sleep.

Jan has also taken on the responsibility for seeing that all the provisions for each leg are up to standard, and will be shooting as much video as possible.

Steve Lloyd

Steve is 43, and was born in Portsmouth. He has known Alan for 26 years, and has been married to Alan's sister Jenette for 21 of those. Steve and Jenette live, with their with two daughters Emma and Kelly, in Lordswood, Southampton, from where Steve commutes to Salisbury every day to work for Concept Interiors.

Steve got into boating sailing a 14 foot clinker-built Cherub, and has partnered Alan on all his RIB events. He does it, like the others, for the 'buzz', a sort of adrenalin addiction, and not surprisingly his family think he's mad.

On the Atlantic trip he will be responsible for the vital fuel load on the boat, involving constant monitoring and balancing of the fuel tanks to enable the boat to run evenly. The boat has a cruising range of about 1200 nautical miles. His most difficult task will be during the crossing to Greenland when the massive ice fields could prevent them from reaching port. If this is the case, fuel management will be crucial.

Also like the rest of the crew, he has complete confidence in his brother-in-law. It never crosses his mind that he won't be coming back.

Vic Palmer

52 years old, Vic was born in Portsmouth and has worked as an engineer for Royal Mail for 26 years, now foreman of the workshop. He is divorced, and has brought up his two boys, Mark and Daren, from when the youngest was about four — he's 26 now. They would both like to be going on the Challenge. Vic lives locally, in Copnor.

He met Alan at Old Portsmouth Airport more than 17 years ago, at a car show where Alan was showing gearboxes and competing, and Vic was scrutineering. He looked at Alan's vehicle and said "Are you going to race that?". "Yes," said Alan." "Well, the prop shaft's about to fall off." So Alan asked if Vic would look at it, and there followed a sporting partnership and friendship which took them through their days as the scourge of the off-road pack, competing in Range Rovers and experimental vehicles, Alan driving and Vic navigating. In 1985 they designed and raced the first rear-engined, semi-automatic gear change off road car. They remember those days with affection.

Vic is a veteran of round Scotland, round Britain, Ireland and the Isle of Wight, and across Biscay. On this trip he is logistics expert, weather man and engineer on the boat, and establishes times of arrival and estimated fuel consumption as well as being secondary navigator. The heaviest of the four, Vic is confident his weight is not going to be a problem as he is training hard on his bicycle and has lost three stone. He has taken the sensible precaution of making a will, but admits he is probably being over-cautious. His confidence in Alan's driving is total. The whole crew's confidence in the backing they have received is total, too.

SEVEN : THE TEAM THAT STAYED BEHIND

Brian Pilcher
Project Manager

Brian Pilcher and Alan Priddy met in the spring of 1996. Brian had been working at Musto for two or three years, and was previously their public relations consultant; Musto also hire him out to other companies, such as Marine Call, the weather forecast people, ITT London & Edinburgh Insurance Company, and a little emerging boat building company. He loves his work.

He has been involved with the boating industry all his working life. He knows media people and they know and trust him. If he says he's going to do something, he does it, and they know it's going to get done. Alan had been using Musto for a long time, and one day said to Brian that he was going to cross the Atlantic, and asked him to handle the public relations. Brian put a proposal to Alan, which he accepted, and since then they have had a warm and relatively successful cooperation. Brian has worked with the press, TV and radio, managing superbly within the restricted budgets available.

His job ends some time after Alan gets back. He is going over to Portsmouth, NH, having already started to fire up the media there, because the best send-off is the best way of getting good value when they come back. It will then be a question of maintaining the flow of information about the trip to the media who are showing an interest, and in that respect he will be covering everything from the Hayling Islander through regional media, to the Press Association, Reuter and the national media. Unfortunately, they are unlikely to take a huge interest in it unless something "interesting" (as Brian puts it — meaning "disastrous") happens. He doesn't want anything too "interesting" to happen, but it would not serve anybody's purpose if they ignored the media until something "interesting" happened — they have to have the background so that if something "interesting" does happen — and it could be something as simple as losing the propeller after hitting ice in the Labrador current somewhere between Labrador and Greenland with visibility at 50 metres — the media are then going to say "Disaster! Our boys are at risk." As Brian says: "If they know the background then hopefully they will see it in the context of a well-organised, properly prepared, well trained expedition rather than four tearaways from Portsmouth, boozing out on the water while their engine isn't working. So it's a question of trying to control that situation, giving the whole thing good credentials."

Brian has ensured there are plenty of good photographs of the crew in the suits and using the equipment. This keeps the sponsors happy. Many photographs, including at a number of little award ceremonies, have already been taken by Portsmouth University photographer Simon Hempsall.

Brian will return from the USA to handle some communications from his office, and then on 11 July he will move down to Portsmouth. The arrangements about the finish and Alan's reception back in Portsmouth he has put in the capable hands of Jerry Wilson of IMS (see next chapter) and a committee of people which includes the City Council and the Yacht Club. Brian expects to be busy with the media and will open up a press office in the Yacht Club with a subsidiary press office in the Bridge Tavern. Much has to be played 'by ear' as a great deal depends on what has happened during the trip. "Nobody in this country's going to get awfully excited about the fact that some little rubber boat has left Portsmouth New Hampshire, but they may start to get excited when we can say our brave boys have left Reykjavik, and have been through shot and shell on the way. It's a tricky balance, keeping people aware of what is happening without boring them to death."

Brian likes to remind people that in France, Italy and Spain RIBs are very popular, and the Mediterranean's north coasts in terms of a market is hugely sophisticated. On the continent, there are more RIBs with cabins, beautiful styling, and water jet engines than there are in the UK. The Italians and French have done with RIBs what they have done with cars — made them desirable, and not just a work boat, which is of course the British attitude.

He is not sure what the media reaction to the crew will be in the UK, realising that we do not tend to lionise sports people in this country, whereas everywhere else in the world, they think they are wonderful. "Sports people are living ordinary people's dreams. They become heroes. The French, for example, have a system in sailing now where anyone who shows promise gets support. Sailing's very popular in French culture."

Brian is most anxious that we in the UK, with our tendency for under-statement, do not under-emphasise what an extraordinary, great feat the Atlantic Challenge is. He is at pains to point out that with the success comes a huge responsibility not to allow people to assume it is easy and, thinking it's easy, go and kill themselves in an attempt to follow in the footsteps of Alan Priddy.

James Priddy

James is Alan's elder son. While Alan is away, he will be manning the command centre in Portsmouth, from where he will send out regular bulletins to sponsors and the media on the progress of *Spirit of Portsmouth*. James is 16, and keen to take on this responsibility.

Having taken his GCSEs this year, James has now left school and is working for his father.

Jerry Wilson

Jerry is a partner, with Richard Finnimore, in IMS (see Chapter 9), who also sponsored the event, but Jerry's involvement with Alan Priddy's adventure is to be more through the Southsea Castle Rotary Club than through work. He has known Alan since they were founder members of their branch of Rotary in 1988. Although he admits to having no desire to 'mess about in boats', he was more than willing, along with Richard, to support Alan in the Round Ireland event already described, where he drove a Landrover as part of the support team, also promoting IMS along the way. He well remembers making the most of the evening rendezvous. One particular day when Alan was several hours late and he and Richard were sitting on the shore worrying, he realised it was his lack of knowledge about the sea which caused the concern. A subsequent ride on the boat on one of the Ireland legs gave Richard more of an insight into the sport, but Jerry has no particular desire to emulate him.

Jerry also worked with Alan on their last Children in Need project, when they built a bridge of boats across the Solent. It is not surprising therefore that Alan, in recognising Jerry's superb organising ability, has asked him to organise their homecoming in July. This will involve drawing together many different involvements — by the Rotary Club, the City Council, sponsors who were to provide equipment, coordination of efforts by police and official timers, as well as organising a collection among the expected large crowds and making available a platform for speeches and presentations to be televised. Jerry will also be organising a barbecue in conjunction with the local yacht club.

Richard Spicer
Commodore, RNC and RAYC

Richard Spicer is Commodore of the combined Royal Naval Club & Royal Albert Yacht Club, based in Old Portsmouth, and as Commodore has responsibility for, and authority over, all sailing activities. Alan contacted him through Musto (Brian Pilcher is an old friend of, and used to work with Richard's Vice Commodore Neil Young, who is in PR as well). Peter Lucas, the Club's chairman at the time was also a friend of Keith Musto — they used to race dinghies together — so everyone knew each other anyway. Richard is involved with the finish of *Spirit of Portsmouth*'s Atlantic run, but has also been heavily involved in the Round the Isle of Wight trial, his first meeting with Alan Priddy. The Club is not normally involved in powerboating, though had been before the war, and is principally involved in sailing.

Richard has been asked to verify that they finish at a certain time. The finish would be visible from the Club if it were not for the intervening buildings at ground level, though members will be able to see the boat coming in towards the finish from an upstairs window. One of Richard's responsibilities is to define the route into Portsmouth, keeping the boat and its undoubted attendant flotilla out of the deep water channel to avoid interference with large vessel routes, and define the finishing line — this will be between Spitsand Fort and a committee boat. The committee boat will be a fully restored high speed launch dating from 1936 — ninety feet long, and an elegant dark blue, it will provide quite literally a finishing touch characteristic of the golden era of powerboating.

A large number of boats are expected in the Solent when *Spirit of Portsmouth* comes home and the tourist board have been alerted to expect crowds on land, too. There will be parking to consider.

Richard will be watching the progress of the Challenge, too. He has put photographs of round the Isle of Wight on the notice board, and also the map of the Atlantic crossing. So the RAYC & RNC will have three involvements in the Challenge — the finish line, as they are RYA-affiliated, and the event has to have that credibility; the invitation to the dignitaries to come and have half a pint of bitter down at the Bridge Tavern is going to be on the Club's headed paper; and third, the helpers are going to be left feeling flat at about half past three or four o'clock in the afternoon, so Richard has suggested there should be a celebration at the Club.

EIGHT : THE RIGHT EQUIPMENT

The Boat • Power and Fuel • Fitting Out • Clothing

Spirit of Portsmouth, Alan Priddy's 7.5 metre rigid inflatable is, of course, not just a boat. Nor is it just a means of transport. It is a survival capsule, with sophisticated systems and many alterations from the standard RIB. During three of the legs, the crew will be out of sight of land for many hours, and any sort of communication will be difficult. They will be entirely on their own.

It is vital, therefore, that *Spirit of Portsmouth* is sturdy, reliable and fully equipped to cope with any conditions the crew may encounter.

Spirit of Portsmouth was built by Ribtec Limited, jointly run by Tim Wilks, at Swanwick (Moody's) Marina, on the A27 east of Southampton, on the River Hamble. The association between Alan Priddy and Ribtec goes back several years.

Ribtec Limited

From the information put out by Ribtec, the company was founded in 1989, and since that time has established a reputation for manufacturing Rigid Inflatable Boats to the most demanding requirements. Already a world-wide supplier of RIBs, the company leads rigid inflatable technology and is renowned for its dedication to quality and customer satisfaction.

The diversity of applications and the demands of commercial and military operators require a flexible approach to RIB construction. Boats can be built in GRP (glass reinforced plastic) or aluminium, with inflatable or flexible closed cell buoyancy tubes. Ribtec is an acknowledged expert in the installation of complex propulsion systems including diesel-waterjet, diesel-stern drive and single or twin outboard engines.

The high quality and performance of Ribtec boats result from attention to detail in the design phase. RIBs are an efficient and safe means of travelling short distances at sea and are used across the spectrum of military, commercial, rescue and recreational roles. Consequently a new design must reflect the operational environment. Ribtec designs are equally suited to the dedicated professional and the enthusiastic amateur. Hull forms are based on a deep 'V' and curved sheer configurations which ensure excellent seaworthiness and safety in the toughest weather conditions.

The company's accumulated experience ensures that the most demanding speed and loading criteria are met with adequate margins at competitive prices.

The construction process starts with the hull and internal mouldings. Each moulding is assembled using premium quality fibreglass mat and resins in a temperature-controlled and humidity-free environment. The ultimate integrity of the hull depends on the maintenance of ideal loading conditions.

Equally important during the initial construction stage is the tube manufacture and its attachment to the hull. Again the working environment is important, requiring close temperature control and dust-free and clinically clean working conditions. Each Ribtec tube is manufactured in Hypalon coated fabric with seam strips inside and out. All tubes are pressure-tested to D.o.T. and international quality standards.

On completion of the tube attachment, Ribtec's craftsmen assemble and fit moulded components, engine, fabrications and accessories to customer requirements. Individual and customised commercial designs undergo rigorous testing before customer acceptance trials and commissioning.

A commitment to quality throughout the production process ensures that the manufacture of all boats is carried out to a high standard The fully-documented quality system records and checks the build quality from design to completion and to recognised international standards.

Ribtec's client list is impressive, and includes HM Coastguard, the Metropolitan Police, the Belgian and Kenyan Navies, and the Royal Yachting Association, and they build RIBs up to 10 metres.

Alan Priddy first approached Tim Wilks in 1990, one year after the start of Ribtec, in response to an advert placed in Practical Boat Owner. Alan had recently completed the first Round Scotland race in a 5 metre RIB and was looking for something more robustly built and purpose-designed. A Ribtec 535 was duly ordered and built and simultaneously Alan expressed interest in a big RIB which was being planned.

Alan Priddy and Jan Falkowski subsequently ordered the first two boats from the newly designed range and tooling commenced.

At this early stage there were just two people actively involved in Ribtec, Tim Wilks and Reg Russell, a former colleague from their previous employment and a man of immense dedication and practical talent. Reg had been employed by Tim's father in 1949 and had stayed with that company, Viking Marine, subsequently Watercraft, up until 1990, when he came to join Tim. Reg was approaching retirement age and was looking for a less stressful environment for his remaining full time employment.

Faced with the problem of designing a new boat and building the plug and mould, Tim approached Alastair Cameron, another former Watercraft colleague, who agreed to supply the design and drawings with the aid of a DTI grant. Reg then suggested to Tim that his son Alan, also a qualified boat builder, may be able to help with the difficult job of building the shape of the new boat in timber from which to make the mould. Alan and Reg Russell subsequently built this critical structure and the first boat was built. This boat has formed the mainstay of Ribtec's production for six years and has proved to be one of the most successful RIBs built.

It should be said that Ribtec would not exist were it not for the tireless efforts of Reg Russell who, during this early life of Ribtec, worked unreasonably long hours for very little reward. His loyalty and dedication to the company laid the foundations for the successful company which Ribtec now finds itself. He now works part time for Ribtec, but his son Alan now manages the workforce of 10.

The RIB has often been dubbed 'The Four Wheel Drive' of the sea, and it is an interesting historical fact that the Land Rover was conceived and pioneered by Maurice and Spencer Wilks, both great uncles of Tim's. It has always been Tim's ambition to emulate the success of that project, and Alan Priddy has done a great deal to reinforce the reputation of the RIB in this respect.

The hull of *Spirit of Portsmouth* was designed by Camarc (Alastair Cameron, who designs all Ribtec's hulls). Alastair is an accomplished patrol and fast boat designer and he worked with Tim in their previous company, Alastair going solo at the same time as Tim. Alan's boat is a standard 7 metre, call a 700. Ribtec normally fit the engines to their boats, but Alan fitted his own.

As far as power for RIBs generally is concerned, there is a huge range of engines available, determined by the customer's speed and distance requirements and load carrying — although there is only a limited number of high speed diesels that can cope with the sort of power that Alan Priddy requires. His size of boat could range from from say 165 hp to 370hp.

RIBs are extremely durable, especially the hull. The tube should last as long, but its life depends on how it is looked after. It is possible to tear it, in which case you repair it with a patch just as you would a puncture in a bicycle tyre. The tube is attached to the hull via a flange, by adhesive. In cross section, it is not unlike a car tyre and, although extremely simple, has been very effective for many years. For example, the RNLI have been using the same principle for decades. By contrast, in the Navy, they tend to use mechanical fastenings.

In the world RIB market, Ribtec have changed considerably since they have been dealing with Alan; nowadays they are very much specialist builders. While they started out building 4 to 6 metre 'run-arounds' and yacht club sailing boats, more recently they have been building almost exclusively larger, special diesel boats, for yacht owners or commercial users like the Port of London.

If somebody asked Ribtec to build a boat similar to Alan Priddy's, just the boat and engine, it would cost somewhere around £28,000.

One of the wonderful things about RIBs is that nothing is needed in the way of spare parts, except for the engine. Tubes can be patched and, since they are in sections, even if part of a tube is destroyed it can be replaced easily and quickly. Alan's tube has five compartments, so in an extreme case he would be able to damage two or even three and still be able to cruise to safety. It was made by Henshaws of Wincanton.

Tim Wilks is no stranger to RIB driving himself, but has very little time for leisure with the business so hectic. He has done some extensive cruising in the past, and some racing — with Alan Priddy, too, who has scared him a few times — but the extreme physical demands are not something he is prepared to take on at the moment. He is, however, supremely confident of the boat's ability to survive the Atlantic crossing, emphasising that the people on board are going to be the ones to suffer.

While the popularity of RIBs worldwide is self-evident, it is difficult to assess the numbers. Tim Wilks believes there are probably two or three times as many enthusiasts as there are owners, because they are still relatively expensive to buy new. However, it is becoming easier to hire them, although there is a certain reluctance by owners to hire them out simply because, like hired four wheel drive vehicles, they tend to be driven hard. But the world market for RIBs is rapidly expanding, and is potentially bigger than the small sailing boat market.

Ribtec cut the deck of Alan's boat apart in 1995 to fit the new fuel tanks. *Spirit of Portsmouth* is the same boat that crossed the Bay of Biscay; only the engine is new. It has bulkheads every two feet, and in the event of flooding there are four pumps, two on and two below the deck.

Ribtec's sponsorship of the Atlantic Challenge has two particularly important facets; first, they are providing the shipping to the USA and, second, they will be there at the finish to carry the boat and it's crew the short journey from Camber Dock to the Bridge Tavern. Tim is keen to see how the boat stands up to the journey. Ribtec's reputation is not exactly riding on it, but he will be keen to see what 4100 miles — and perhaps contact with ice — will do to the boat.

It may come as a surprise to some people that Yamaha, famous for its motorcycles and its aspirations in Formula 1 motor racing, makes marine diesel engines.

Yamaha Motor (UK) Limited

The engine powering *Spirit of Portsmouth* is a Yamaha ME370 STI diesel out-drive. It is a turbo-charged and water cooled four-stroke unit developing 165 bhp, and will power the boat at 40 knots, using only 1 litre of fuel per nautical mile. According to the manufacturer's specifications, the base engine is an in-line 4 cylinder Toyota model, with a total capacity of 3660 cc and a compression ratio of 16.5:1.

The coolant is sea water drawn in through the drive unit, filtered and circulated by a pump.

The turbo-charger is an important feature. Common problems with conventional turbo-chargers are lack of power and delay in acceleration in the low and middle engine speed range, due to low exhaust pressure. To get around these limitations, Yamaha has used a very compact, lightweight turbine with small diameter blades. The results of this innovation are greatly improved acceleration, smooth and quick charge pressure increase, smoother and more comfortable operation and reduced engine stress.

Yamaha's Hydra Drive provides smooth, effortless shifting; a unique hydraulic multi-plate clutch system guarantees positive gear engagement. The 18 inch propeller is stainless steel with a 46° tilt range, and steering (up to 60°) is power-assisted hydraulically.

The whole power unit has a high level of warning systems and the full range of comprehensive instruments. Alan can confirm that the unit has easy access to servicing components, yet it is extremely compact at 729 mm wide, 492 mm high and 1073 mm long, and a total weight, including the drive, of just 490 kg. Above all, it provides 'petrol' performance with diesel reliability and economy. Battery charging is by high output 80 amp alternator.

I doubt if many people will want to read any more technical information than this, but anyone who does is welcome to contact Yamaha's Marine Technical Representative Joe Poulter, who kindly provided the technical details I have included. Joe is based at Brooklands, in Surrey.

Fuel is directly injected into the engine by high pressure rotary pump, and the electrical fuel lift pump has a manual override switch. Standard fitting includes a water contamination warning system.

There are three integral fuel tanks below the sole: 22 gallon (100 litre) forward, 18 gallon (80 litre) aft, and 31 gallon (140 litre) in the main central tank. She will also carry two 55 gallon (250 litre) flexible tanks which will lie just inside the tubes wedged in between the engine compartment and the console. All fuel is pumped by electronics with a manual override in the event of failure, and at speed a good trim is vital.

With the spare 132 gallon (600 litre) flexible tank that they also have on board, they actually have the range to go straight from Nova Scotia to Ireland. But as Alan Priddy rightly comments, there would be little point in bobbing along at sea for five days. It would be excruciatingly boring. The object is to go from port to port, meet people, have a few beers and see "what's going down". The crew need refuelling as much as the Yamaha engine.

The flexible tanks are built by Air Cushion Ltd of Marchwood and are flexible — they can be rolled up when not in use. They may be needed for the longer legs, or in order to salvage diesel if there is a fuel leak in one of the other tanks. Alan anticipates stopping about every four hours or 100 miles for refuelling at sea.

The boat will have a top speed of 42 knots, but until half the fuel is burnt off, she will only reach 35 knots. The whole trip has been planned at between 22 and 25 knots for safety.

Fitting out

The cockpit controls were fitted by Alan and, while some are supplied with the engine, it is a matter of personal choice where they are sited. The controls and read-outs include engine oil pressure, engine temperature, compass, propeller position gauge, computer diagnostic panel, revolutions counter and engine hour gauge, global position read-out from 13 satellites, gearbox trim switch, fresh air vent, electronic map system, electronic fuel gauge, radio, battery level gauge, speed, distance and outside water temperature. The console is more akin to a light aircraft's than a powerboat.

Navigation equipment consists of two GPSs and one chart plotter, one radar scanner and one conventional compass. All navigation will be done before leaving and flip-type pages will be used on board throughout the trip. All the charts for the trip will be sealed in a waterproof tank for use in the event of emergencies.

Alan is hoping the boat will be carrying a Sat Com, not only to keep in touch with the media, but for emergency use. Emergency EPIRBS will be carried personally, and the flexible tanks will double up as life rafts should it be necessary to abandon ship. They will also carry a collapsible mast and sail system in the improbable event of total engine failure. For the trip, the boat will be fitted with a bow canopy (doubling as the sail), not only to carry advertising but to provide valuable shelter for two crew in the coldest conditions. Hot air from the engine compartment will not only keep the bilge and fuel tanks warm, but can be ducted through the front locker into the canopy to warm the air inside for comfort.

Heavy duty reinforcement fabric has been applied to the underside of the hull to protect her from damage by submerged ice. One last item of safety equipment stored in the boat, to be dumped overboard before they arrive in England, will be a rifle. Polar bears are not particularly friendly, and they are usually hungry.

The interior layout of the boat was also custom-made to fit this particular crew. The seating arrangement is a standard two in front and two in tandem behind; both of the rear seats are classed as resting seats, built of high density foam to minimise shock waves travelling through the body when resting.

There will be a small cooking stove to boil water for hot drinks. The plan is that when they stop they will have several vacuum flasks full of hot water and while they are drinking or eating, replacement water will be brewing. The crew themselves will be carrying very few personal effects; there will not be room. A small bag each will contain their few essentials: a change of clothes and a toilet bag for when they go ashore. In the console they will each have stowed a sleeping bag and a survival bag with flares and rations.

It is something of an eye-opener to see to what extent a basic RIB can be adapted. It is worth emphasising that if a RIB can be fitted out to go where *Spirit of Portsmouth* is going, it can be fitted out to go absolutely anywhere.

On a voyage such as this, though, it is not enough to have an efficiently-powered boat which will get you reliably from one port to another. Whatever else it may be, it is still an open boat, and the occupants have to be able to withstand the elements. Temperatures can drop to -40° when wind chill factor is taken into account. Water is everywhere, and you would probably not survive a dip. Just staying dry is not a question of comfort in the polar regions; it is a matter of life or death, and the historical problem with a suit that kept liquid out was that it kept liquid in. This may sound perverse, but the body can expire several pints of liquid in a day, much of it through the skin, and it is therefore essential that this liquid is not trapped inside the clothing, defeating the object of the dry suit.

The crew of *Spirit of Portsmouth* will not have this problem; they will be wearing Musto clothing.

Musto Limited

Keith Musto, Olympic silver medallist, originally made sails for a living but, being a sailor himself, diversified into making clothing out of sheer frustration at the lack of suitable clothing on the market. Musto Limited celebrated its 25th anniversary in 1996. For some years they have been able to claim that their clothing gives the best protection in the world, thanks to their performances in Whitbread Round the World Races and the confidence in Musto expressed by the world's leading ocean sailors. Their capability in design and manufacture has won market leadership and, even more important, a reputation of which they can be proud. It is a reputation not only for innovation, but reliability, durability and comfort — a vital factor at 3 am on a cold, wet, windy morning.

Musto clothing is highly sophisticated, durable and lightweight. It's also stylish and, as is the case with trainers being worn by most non-sportsmen, Musto clothing is often a fashion accessory worn by people who live near — or want to be seen in — the world's most up-market marinas and resorts worldwide.

Crews on the BT Global Challenge have relied on Musto HPX systems throughout the worst and best of the world's weather, and with some 280 crew wearing it, the system has clocked up more than 8 million sea miles. It's not surprising, therefore, that this should be the first choice of clothing for the challenge across the North Atlantic. Even in midsummer, the North Atlantic and the ice-strewn waters of Labrador, Greenland and the Denmark Strait are notable for their inhospitability. Remote from the benign influence of the Gulf Stream, the crew will have freezing temperatures, fog banks and the risk of collision with icebergs to contend with and will demand clothing which is designed to withstand the assault of freezing rain, spray and extreme wind chill levels.

So what is so special about Musto clothing? It is in the combination of materials. The Musto 3-layer Clothing System consists of an HPX breathable, waterproof one-piece suit which conceals a middle layer with a deep fibre pile to provide warmth to the body and limbs, and the additional thermal protection of a high performance underwear layer made from Polartec 100. The middle layer salopettes have a two-way zip, hand-warmer pockets and protective knee and seat patches. The outer layer is very light and soft, and constructed of nylon. The middle Gore-tex™ membrane has 9 billion pores per square inch, and inside is another nylon layer to protect the inside of the Gore-tex.

Not only does the Musto System keep you warm, it enables perspiration (everyone sweats, even in low temperatures) to be whisked away from the skin and transpired to the atmosphere. Driving at anything up to 40 knots in low temperatures means that feet, hands and head must also be perfectly protected to prevent wind chill or even frostbite. It is not surprising that this is the company to which the RNLI turn for protection of the country's lifeboat volunteers. The system also comes with a 'drop seat' system designed to make trips to the toilets faster, safer and more convenient.

Alan Priddy has been a Musto fan for years, but the new breathable system has impressed him; he recognises that in RIB driving you expect to have fun, but you don't expect to be comfortable, but that Musto have gone a long way to change all that. When he got back to Portsmouth from Bilbao after 35 hours afloat, he unzipped and took off his dry suit feeling tired but fresh. The 700 mile trial had convinced the crew that Musto HPX would be the right clothing system for the Atlantic trek.

The yellow foul weather gear — an all-in-one dry suit — is made of new Gore-Tex membrane which is lightweight and durable. Because it is fully breathable, it can be worn for weeks on end. It has seals at the neck and wrists, and when you put it on, air is trapped inside. The quantity of air you want to have inside is a personal choice — too much air can be expelled by inserting a finger into the neck seal, making a gap, then bending down to squeeze out some of the air. Too little, and more air can be introduced through a mouth-operated valve. The feet of the suit are integral, and will fit inside footwear. Rather than boots, which would take up too much space, the crew are using cheap, thick-soled trainers to insulate their feet from the deck. They have chosen not to wear helmets because of the strain they put on the neck, and have opted for Musto hard hat tops and goggles.

There will be two life jackets for each crew member, and each will carry a personal electronic beacon (identical to the one that drew rescuers to stranded yachtsman Tony Bullimore).

The suits will probably go back to Musto to be inspected after the voyage. What they will be looking for are things which may be related particularly to long-distance RIB driving. While movement creates chafing, which can ultimately allow water in, Musto are confident this will not happen — the miles of testing in extreme sailing conditions suggest they should stand up to 4000 miles of powerboating. Any unforeseen areas of wear can be put right before the system is offered to other RIB drivers around the world. Similarly, if sitting in one position for long periods identifies any area of discomfort, such as a crease in the wrong place, then that can be adjusted too.

Musto are happy for their suits to be tested in this public way and emphasise that it is not only being seen that is important, but being seen to be listening to their customers.

NINE : THE SPONSORS, SUPPORTERS AND BENEFICIARIES

Most, if not all of the people in this section will be strangers to readers of this book. But please don't skip it — they are all integral to the story. In fact, without the contributions of many of them, the Atlantic Challenge would have been difficult, if not impossible, to achieve.

Although Chapters Five and Eight have already gone into some detail regarding equipment and planning, you will see from this chapter that there were still things which have not been covered elsewhere, and would be considered desirable or even essential to anyone undertaking a long sea journey by RIB.

Sponsors and supporters are listed alphabetically and, though the notes on each vary in length, they are all equally important to the project.

Air Cushion of Marchwood
provided the flexible fuel tanks.

Allan & Bath
residential letting agents, have pledged financial support.

Concept Interiors

Steve Lloyd works for, and is sponsored by Concept Interiors. The original company formed in February 1988 when Jeff Sharpe and Phil Kimber joined forces to become a partnership operating out of a water mill in Romsey, Hampshire, specialising in commercial flooring installations. Steve joined the company shortly after the initial setting up and his experience with carpet fitting and floor laying helped the company get established.

The company has high praise for him: "Steve Lloyd has been an invaluable member of staff not only in his workmanship but sense of humour, which has stood him in good stead especially when we needed him to work 24 to 30 hours at a stretch on contracts such as Woolworth's store refurbishments."

Concept Interiors have over the years sponsored all the RIB events Steve and Alan have been involved in, and have great pleasure in wishing Steve and the team a safe and successful journey this time, and hope: "...that Steve will still enjoy ICE in his gin and tonic after the event!"

T Couzens & Sons Ltd

builders of West Marden, have pledged financial support.

Devonshire Estates

are providing financial and moral support to the event.

Mayor of Portsmouth, Eileen Foley, and the People of Portsmouth, NH

Full support has been pledged. Portsmouth will be hosting the start of the Challenge, which will be a major event in the city's calendar.

Gales Brewery

will provide a lorry for the band at the end of the voyage.

Garth Henry, Bangor

Garth has plans to meet *Spirit of Portsmouth* with hot coffee and real food when they make their first landfall back in the UK.

Henshaw Inflatables Ltd

Henshaws built the rigid inflatable tube. They were nearly listed under "Enshaws" until Alan told me that he had inadvertently scraped the initial H off the sponsor's name on the hull of the boat...

Hilsea Engineers

helped with fitting out *Spirit of Portsmouth*.

IMS

Integrated Manufacturing Systems operate from offices in Southampton and Rotherham, and offer a full range of products and services from project management to disaster recovery. Their flagship product, Uniplan, is a fully integrated business management system to give companies, irrespective of size, effective computerised control of both production and finance. Specialist staff are employed with proven experience in systems, manufacturing and cost accounting.

Jerry Wilson of IMS is playing a key role in fund raising for this event and also taking care of the home-coming arrangements.

IMS are sponsoring the magnificent glass trophy to be presented to Alan and his crew at the finish.

Lyndhurst School

In Crofton Road, North End, Portsmouth, Lyndhurst School has given a project to follow the course of the Atlantic Challenge to a group of pupils: Daniel Beck, Tom Cannell, Emma Dingwall, James Eaton, Rebecca Eastman, Sarah Gardner, James Gregory, Ashley Harris, Charlotte Hember Kamlesh Kaur, Joseph MacDonald, Catherine May, Ashley Restell and Daniel Savigar have a large map to follow when the challenge takes place, and they have met the crew and been for a ride in the boat.

Shaun McKenna and the crew from Wentworth Marina
will be providing weather information and facilities prior to the start.

Beatrice Marconi and family
are looking after the crew during their stay in Portsmouth, NH.

Per Neilson (Nanortalik) and Air Base
are providing Arctic weather and ice reports for the crew.

Peters and May
are the shipping agents handling the movement of the boat in the USA.

Portsmouth City Council (England)
has pledged full help and support for the project.

Portsmouth Royal Mail Social Club
are providing financial and moral support

Priority Stainless
have supplied vital fittings for the boat.

Rosemead Developments
have pledged financial support.

Jonathan Smith
is the journalist most closely in touch with events throughout.

Southsea Castle Rotary
are working hard on fund raising for the event, and the homecoming.

Travel Planners
arranged the crew's flights.

Val and Mike Verlander
are taking delivery of the boat when it arrives in the USA.

Wallaneus
shipped the boat and did their job magnificently.

White Light
supplied films to the crew.

There were only two major disappointments. After being party to the launch of their system at the London Boat Show, Alan Priddy was regrettably unable to persuade Magellan to lend a satellite communicator for the voyage, which would have meant schools, families, the general public and the media would have had live access to the crew on route, and the crew would have had an on board e-mail facility. With hindsight, the two emergencies might have been less fraught with the system on board, but the problem appeared to be the risk of damage to the new equipment.

The other disappointment was that significant TV coverage was put out of the question owing to failure to secure an on board broadcast-quality video recording system.

THE BENEFICIARIES

The Cancer Care Society

The Cancer Care Society was pioneered by George Poole in 1971 (as the Cancer Aftercare and Rehabilitation Society). It was the first cancer support charity of its kind, and over the years has developed a national network of groups, a telephone link system, a counselling service, resources, information and holiday accommodation for families. It is also aiming to set up a chain of Centres and currently has three — two in Wales (Merthyr Tydfil and Neath) and one in Romsey, Hampshire. The Centres are open six days a week and each has a professional counsellor and centre coordinator and a back-up team of trained voluntary workers.

In 1969, George was treated for cancer. Through his own experience of isolation he realised the value of sharing feelings with other cancer patients. After his recovery George was determined to help other people by sharing his own experience and, from the small beginning, emotional and practical support has been given to many thousands of people. Today, with the confident backing of professionals working in this field of medicine, the demand for the service is increasing daily. Continued financial support is crucial to the development and expansion of the Society.

People can help the Society in a number of ways — by volunteering to provide befriending and practical help for the many people who contact the CCS, by setting up a local support group, by publicising the details of their work through the media, library displays, and so on, and by providing holiday facilities. Of course, financial support is always needed, which can be through donations, deeds of covenant, salary deductions and large or small fund raising events.

The Cancer Care Society is a Registered Charity (No.263899).

Alan Priddy took up Steve Lloyd's suggestion to make the Cancer Care Society the beneficiary of the Atlantic Challenge: "For my crew and I, in our 7.4 metre open inflatable, the Trans-Atlantic, west to east, is 'The Big One'. The charity we have chosen is also fighting 'The Big One' in its own field."

Increasingly, the tide is turning in favour of the patient, with long remissions or even complete recovery being achieved. During the fight, caring support is vital. Needless to say, in cases where cancer is the victor, counselling, understanding, sympathy and love must continue long after the battle is lost.

TEN : COUNTDOWN

The final shakedown for the Atlantic Challenge is booked for April, when the crew of *Spirit of Portsmouth* will attempt to circumnavigate the Isle of Wight a record number of times in 24 hours. They are going anti-clockwise. The principal purpose of this is to test the new Yamaha engine and the boat in her new trim.

On April 4 the boat is blessed by the Bishop of Portsmouth. The following day, at midday, they set off under the eye of the Royal Albert Yacht Club and Royal Naval Club. 2 hours, 10 minutes later, they have completed the 60 mile lap, logged by the Club. For twelve hours they continue at the same pace. 5 laps completed.

At about 1230 that night, the Coastguard radios an imminent storm warning. The crew ask: "When?" The answer is: *"Now."* "What strength?" *"7. Maybe 8."* "What direction?" *"South westerly."* A pause. "We'll go round one more time." *"I don't think you will."*

It takes 2 hours 15 minutes to travel 17 miles. It is horrendous. They have chosen the 5th because of a full moon, but now low cloud is coming down, nil visibility, force 7 gale. There is nothing for it but to deploy all the safety gear and lie-to. Eventually it takes 6 hours, 10 minutes to complete the 6th lap.

The rules for the Isle of Wight record say if you cross the finishing line it is the start of another lap, and if you don't finish that lap by the end of the 24 hour period you are deemed to be a non-finisher. As they have started at midday they have to cross the finishing line at midday.

Coming past Bembridge at 7 in the morning it is still blowing a gale and they decide they will not get round in the 5 hours remaining. There is nothing for it but to drift in the Solent until midday. For 5 hours. They are offered cups of tea. They must refuse. They are offered sandwiches, and even a tow. They must refuse. It's the rules.

But the trophy is theirs, and a magnificent trophy. The media coverage is excellent, and the Daily Mirror has picked it up. Now everyone is talking about the Atlantic Challenge.

The shakedown is a success. The engine is superb. The trim is excellent. Now all they have to do is pack the boat up and ship it off to America? Not quite; there are still half a million things to do. And the clock is running.

ELEVEN : FIT AND READY?

First there is the question, on a 600 mile open sea leg, of bodily functions. In a one piece suit, in temperatures of minus 10°. It is not on. Face the fact that you probably have 36 to 48 hours to wait before seeing your next water closet. You can take a couple of pills which will block your bowels for 48 hours, then take another pill which will unblock them. Problem solved. But it is the least of their problems.

Wes Hart at Portsmouth University has developed a regime for Alan Priddy and Steve Lloyd to ensure they are fully fit for the voyage. Wes is a personal trainer, and he has been in the boat to get some idea of what the physical problems are going to be.

Exercise regimes are difficult enough to make sport-specific, and this is more difficult than most.

Jan is making his own arrangements, but Wes takes Alan quietly aside and recommends he does not take Vic. Vic is the first to admit he is not fit, his blood pressure is high and his weight is going to make it difficult for him to get fit. But if he is nothing else, Vic is determined, and he cycles every day and does his best to lose weight by dieting. The rest of the crew discuss it. They have always been together; they will stay together, and support Vic, no matter what. The fact that none of them could lift him, if it were necessary, is not mentioned.

Alan, Vic and Steve begin their fitness regime on 14 November. The press are there for the weigh-in. It is going to be hard.

Plans are setting. Alan, Vic and Brian Pilcher will fly out on Friday 13 June, drive up to Maine where boat is, recommission the boat and have a 10-day break. Recommissioning will only take one day, because Wallaneus, the Southampton shipping line have agreed to ship the boat complete. The journey will take 21 days.

The person Alan has been dealing with at Battle Harbour has gone missing. Alan manages to track down Keith Poole, his replacement, and is now in negotiations for their accommodation — so far it is board and lodging for the crew for however long, in exchange for a day's work on the project.

Everything is set in Nova Scotia, and the crew is scheduled to be there on 23 June, which is the actual day John Cabot sighted Newfoundland.

There is still no contact with anyone in Greenland, although they have established they should be able to get fuel at the fishing manager's office, because there is a fish factory there. Speaking to people in Nova Scotia (Natalie Marsh), and Battle, the seaways are iced in at the moment.

It has been a particularly hard winter up there. The problem is, if they cannot go as far north as they need to go, they have little choice but to go across the Atlantic non-stop — from Labrador to Iceland. Unassisted and on a wing and a prayer. It remains a contingency plan.

Alan is keeping in touch with local people, mostly fishermen, to check on the ice situation. He is not complimentary about weather forecasters. He has got to know an Icelandic family, some members of whom are living in Southampton. They have offered accommodation in Iceland.

A command centre is being set up in Alan's office where he can fax bulletins for dissemination to families and the media.

Alan is trying to persuade BT to loan a Satcom. They will still have a satellite locator, but will not be able to talk on it.

Saturday, 12 July for the finish is set in stone. The Portsmouth City Council are behind it now, and The (Portsmouth) News is planning feature articles — a double page spread before they go with cut-outs of the boat, one during the voyage of their progress, but also something on the top of the front page every day. Brian is responsible for media contact and is getting interest from the dailies. Radio 5 want to do live interviews in every stopover by land line . Filming at sea depends on TV companies at the ports — they will get plenty of notice — the crew is prepared to do a dummy filming run. Alan is trying through local contacts to locate the nearest ISDN lines to wherever they stop so they can download the photos they've taken — vital for the media.

Meanwhile, Alan complains the fitness regime is killing him. He has muscles in his body where he didn't think he could have muscles — his legs are incredibly strong; he can feel muscles bulging even when he is sitting down. And they now want him to train harder — still doing 3 mornings a week, but instead of 45 minutes, an hour. He thinks, oh, only 15 minutes more. But that's the killer.

They are all doing different, tailored, exercises now. Vic has lost two stone, but is shouted at for putting some back on. It is so easy to get in the car instead of riding the bike to work. He will probably lose another stone, and then another on the trip. But he then may have to take supplements for short term weight loss.

Alan is getting nowhere trying to raise interest from an American charity. Alan is disparaging. Typical Americans. Laid back. Do it later. But the Mayor of Portsmouth, NH, Eileen Foley, has taken it under her wing and has a committee on it, so something should happen.

Three English schools are interested in linking with one in New

Hampshire — Lyndhurst, Marchwood and Romsey. Alan would like them to do a project on the Internet between them, if possible.

There is no luck yet setting up a web page. Time is running short. The Cancer Care Society are finding it difficult to put much time into the project. But the idea is not just for charity. Alan says with a smile he's doing it for himself, to raise his profile in the marine industry and media, so when he decides to call it a day he can earn a living as a consultant. Is this one of those unguarded moments?

A Radio Solent interviewer suggests the crew are too old to be doing this. Alan bites his lip and restrains himself.

They have spent too much time on the boat over the winter, Alan has decided. There comes a point at which you are not going to make it any safer or any more reliable. They exceeded that point by at least 10%.

The boat is ready. It has power. It has a mast and a sail — it might do 3 or 4 knots with that. Three of the crew are sailors. There are paddles. People have rowed across before. What more can be done?

Alan is still hopeful of TV coverage by remote camera on board and wiring the crew for sound with voice-activated microphones or radio helmets. Part of the purpose of the trip is to test new equipment. If anyone wants to give the crew a piece of practical and relevant kit, they will use it. The word is out to most of the marine industries via the Southampton and London boat shows.

Ribtec have generously offered to ship the boat to America. A watercolourist friend of Alan's in Belgium has agreed to put a picture together with all the components of the trip, which will be sold at auction, and used for the cover of the souvenir issue of the newsletter. They are looking at other revenue from goods such as caps and T-shirts.

The Guinness Book of Records have agreed to accept the voyage as a world record provided it can be verified. There are three possible world records on the cards — [1] the total elapsed time by a RIB across the Atlantic, [2] the fastest aggregate sea time, started by the US Coastguard and finished and restarted by every harbour master and [3] the longest and highest latitude journey done by a RIB — this one is not yet accepted, but the other two are. [3] would be a new record — no-one has done it before. Well, Erik the Red has — but can he prove it?

Alan is still trying to get permission to use the satellite communicator. It doesn't officially exist. He hopes to be able to do interviews from the boat. He has agreed with IBM that there will be a satellite link with Portsmouth High School, so getting the community involved.

Back-up equipment has to be considered. The boat actually weighs one and a half tons, but will weigh about three tons when they set out, and about 2 tons at the finish. Cruising is wetter for the crew when the boat is full of fuel, and it's a different driving technique. The aim is an average of 22 to 25 knots, meaning top speeds of over 30 knots when conditions permit. That means there will be little capacity for back ups.

The author is pestering. Whose idea was it to write a book? What sort of wave size can you cope with? Does a long swell make it easier? Do you have to stop if it's foggy? In what sort of sea conditions would you not make any headway?

If you have run down a wave, you have to drive back up, and if you lose momentum you have to run with that wave. If the waves are running in your direction, you just pitch the forward speed with the run of the sea.

If it's foggy, it's not windy, therefore it's flat. If it's windy, it's going to be more difficult. If it's foggy, the radar will work better, so there are compensations.

Not making headway in bad sea conditions is not probably not relevant. They would have a satellite image of the journey, and would know the weather conditions. Even on a 600 mile journey, it's not likely to catch them unawares, because of the speed they are travelling, and because they have an indication of what the weather's going to do over a 24 hour period. They may be 48 hours on some trips, but if the weather is good, then they can do the legs quite quickly. If the weather is bad, then they look at the 48 hour pattern. There are no interim emergency stopovers planned. They seem to have all the answers. Alan doesn't say "pass" once.

While cruising, the crew are not strapped in, but the person who is asleep will have a lap strap. He will sleep sitting upright — if you're tired, you'll sleep anywhere, catnapping. Anybody can stay awake for 24 hours if they've had the occasional half-hour or so of sleep. They ran a test in 1996 on alertness in the boat, and found that after 23 hours, things start to go wrong. But after half an hour top-up of sleep, you can go on for 30 hours. Another half hour — 48 hours. But not more than that.

So if they were at sea for a long time and the weather wasn't favourable, and they were getting over-tired, that would be the time to put out the sea anchor out and go to sleep for an hour. All of them. The chances of getting mown down by a ship would be remote, especially with an audible warning on the radar.

It is May, 1997. There are only a quarter of a million things left to do. But it's too late to back out now. The boat has gone.

TWELVE : SPRING 1997 : TOO LATE TO BACK OUT NOW

Wes Hart of Portsmouth University Fitness Department has gone to Vietnam; Alan doesn't take it personally — if they are not fit now…

At the eleventh hour they are offered a useless filming opportunity. The boat has already gone and the offer does not include going out to the USA to fit the system to the boat. In the end, it is Jan's father's who comes up with a video camera.

Alan Priddy is already talking about the next event. He knows people think it's mad, but he just likes toying with the idea of finding out whether something can be done.

The boat has disappeared. The shippers inform him there is a problem getting the trailer on to the road because it is not registered in the USA. A nine days' worry. Alan thinks it is all over before it has begun.

The Greenland stage of the voyage is the most unpredictable and Alan has packed six bottles of whisky to use as barter if they need supplies at Nanortalik, the most remote stop.

It will be a double worry for Liz Binnall, Alan's partner, after he sets off from Portsmouth USA on Sunday. Vying for her attentions during his voyage will be her 15 year old daughter, Leah, who is on an alpine adventure holiday, mountain climbing and white water rafting while Alan crosses the Atlantic. Liz will not be relying on regular updates, having learned from the Bilbao-Portsmouth event that it's better not to expect news. She has been through it several times before and always worries. They don't set a time for phone calls because, if he can't get in touch, she will only think the worst. The secret of their six year relationship is freedom for them both to pursue their own goals. She is studying for her City and Guilds in upholstery and interior design at South Downs College, Havant. She is not going to the USA to see him off — she has an exhibition at college to take part in.

The itinerary can be published now —

Leg	Approximate:	Land miles	Nautical miles	Expected duration (hrs)
Portsmouth to Nova Scotia		620	538	24
Sydney to Labrador		650	564	24
Labrador to Greenland		700	608	30
Greenland to Iceland		800	695	35
Iceland to Northern Ireland		750	651	30
Northern Ireland to Portsmouth		530	460	20

The crew of Spirit of Portsmouth: Left to right: Jan Falkowski, Alan Priddy, Vic Palmer and Steve Lloyd

Portsmouth, USA: Two police officers, Vic Palmer, John Bohenko (City Manager), Alan Priddy, Mike Pendleton (US Coastguard) and colleague have all given their approval to the departure

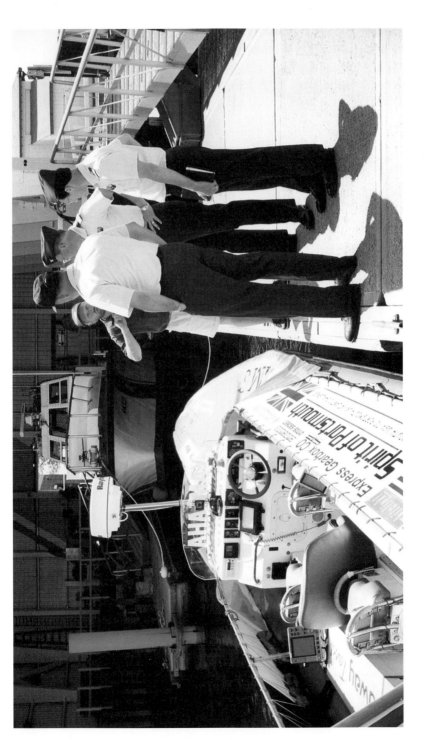

Portsmouth, USA: Alan discussing final arrangements with Marine Safety Agency officers

Portsmouth, USA: Some of the many friends made here, including Jeanie Wentworth and her husband

Portsmouth, USA: Eileen Foley, Mayor

Portsmouth, USA: Away at last

North Sydney, Nova Scotia: Steve anxiously smokes a cotton bud while Vic performs major surgery on the radar

North Sydney, Nova Scotia: Review and drying out of kit at the end of Leg One

Charts, schedules, forecasts, contacts and other information are all together. Some have been laminated for durability.

Alan is still wearing his PR hat. He tells the media he is prepared, and if their efforts help to overcome the threat of cancer — surely the big shadow over so many lives — their endeavours will not be in vain.

By 16 May, he has news from Greenland at last — he has made contact with Per Nielson who owns the hotel in Nanortalik. Per speaks good English and has given Alan his phone and fax number, and will look out of the window to see what the ice situation is like 24 hours before *Spirit of Portsmouth* leaves Labrador. As of yesterday, he informs Alan the harbours are still iced up but should be clear in late June. In answer to Alan's last question — yes, he does drink whisky.

They are learning about ice. A big iceberg is called a growler. They will find out why. It is icebergs less than 5 square metres, "bergy bits", that are the ones to watch out for — they are the ones which could damage the boat.

Alan is a believer in Murphy's Law (anything that can go wrong, will go wrong). He has considered all its implications. The worst that can happen is that they can die (he hopes they don't); they can get lost (with GPS that will be difficult); they can hit ice (they will have radar); they can break down (they will have to repair it); they might not be able to get provisions or sufficient fuel to carry on (that would be a shame). What matters, he says, is having faith in one's ability to survive. Fear is healthy as long as it doesn't overcome you. Alan does not feel comfortable up a ladder — it is all relative.

Even now Alan will still drive down to the seafront at lunchtime to see the sea. The wave patterns have a fascination for him, especially in the equinox months.

It is obviously a time for reflection. Alan considers himself as much an adventurer as explorer, but just as important is being friendly. He is happy just to turn up somewhere and have a nice meal and generally socialise with new people. Turning up at a remote fishing village where people talk to you is becoming harder to do. You have to travel further. It doesn't matter to Alan how far.

He is looking forward to the companionship, too. Vic has always been at his side whenever things have gone wrong. He could not imagine it being otherwise. Steve and he are like brothers, and Alan laughs when Jan is mentioned. All he will say is that Jan is in the right profession. The four of them are a true team — voices might be raised under pressure, but they do not fight. It makes all the difference.

Vic, Brian Pilcher and Alan fly to the USA on 13 June. The rest of the crew will join them the following Wednesday. They are looking forward to their reception locally. There is an immediate hitch. Virgin will not let them board the aircraft with one-way tickets to the USA. Whether it is against Virgin's policy or the US Immigration rules is not clear, and the crew find themselves in the ridiculous situation of having to buy return tickets in order to get on the flight. They are promised a refund — some time.

Val (Alan's sister) and Mike Verlander in Maine welcome them warmly. They take delivery of the boat, and proceed to put it in order. Some items are missing — electronic equipment and prescription sunglasses at least. Alan is devastated. Fearing the voyage is going to end in Maine, Alan contacts Raytheon Marine for replacements and the President gives instructions to his staff — whatever they want — give it to them. It is front page news from Boston right the way up to Bangor. Raytheon of course get good coverage, and are in the news anyway, having just paid $18 billion for the Hughes Aircraft Corporation.

The next hitch is a literal one. The trailer cannot be towed from Maine to Portsmouth because it is not licensed to travel on US roads. Alan is fed up. With typical decisiveness, he sells the trailer to the local marina for a dollar so they can put the marina's licence plates on it. They are on the way to the start line.

There is a warm welcome waiting for them. The people of Portsmouth NH find them an odd bunch — wacky, crazy and just plain mad — is how they describe Alan Priddy's trans-Atlantic adventure. The adventurers became a regular sight alongside the exclusive Wentworth Marina where the wealthy Americans play with their boats. Many of them seldom take to the water, preferring to party while game-fishing craft are safely moored to the concrete pontoons. Alan, Jan, Steve and Vic become a regular sight in the pubs and restaurants of this naval city — now considered the fifth best place to live in the US.

Marina owner Paul Holloway is insistent the crew have captured the hearts of the people of Portsmouth. No one can believe they are going across the Atlantic in 'that little boat'. Boat owner Kathy Rush says everyone is talking about the eccentric Englishmen. She believes people are interested — excited — because they wish they had the guts to do it.

In the evening they take delivery of a large quantity of doughnuts, kindly donated by a lady with a doughnut franchise who Alan has met in a car park, sporting a new Mustang convertible which she has just won for a dollar. They store the doughnuts in the boat.

They have permission to leave the USA. They had filed the passage plan with the US Coastguard in Boston via Commander Mike Pendleton of the Portsmouth Coastguard in the previous October. Mike had heard nothing, and assumed approval would be granted. The boat had been inspected by the US equivalent of the Marine Safety Agency — who thought it highly amusing, but couldn't find anything wrong with the boat. The Coastguard say they will definitely start the Challenge off on the Sunday at midday because they want to make sure the boat leaves — that way the Canadians would have to take responsibility... Alan believes they jest.

Beatrice Marconi, who has been looking after the crew during their stay in Portsmouth, has (unknown to the crew at the time) been preparing to run for mayor of the city. She and her family host a farewell barbecue on their last day ashore, June 21. Later, they are in the bar. Jonathan Smith of the The News (Portsmouth, Hampshire) has joined them, and Alan is talking about where they will go next. Suggestions come pouring in — retracing the journeys of the American clippers around Cape Horn — New York to San Francisco — seemed favourite. This route would pit the rigid inflatable against the heavy seas and winds — known as the roaring forties — that rush through the gap between Antarctica and the tip of South America. A trip round Australia is discounted because of the long distance the crew would face between coastal towns (and the consequent lack of pubs). London to Monte Carlo, and Newport, Rhode Island to Bermuda were also suggested, as well as a dash across the Bering Straits between Siberia and Alaska. New York to San Francisco via a northern route was ruled out because of the permanent polar ice.

Alan is asked why he starts thinking about new challenges before this one is even completed. His answer is simple — there are still many places he hasn't been. And more than anything, he enjoys meeting the people and seeing the look on their faces when he tells them where he's come from... and how he arrived.

Vic looks on in disbelief. Shaking his head, he goes to bed.

THIRTEEN : LEG ONE

Portsmouth, New Hampshire to Nova Scotia

Day 1 : Sunday, June 22, 1997

It's very hot. 110°. To prove their loyalty to one of their main sponsors, put on their thermal clothing. Brian Pilcher is quite adamant they are going to walk out in front of the TV cameras in the all-singing, all-dancing kit. They are sorry they don't have a suit for Brian to wear; they feel like astronauts walking to the rocket. Among the many, many well-wishers is the President of Raytheon, Robert Ungers, and the crew appreciate his gesture in joining them for their leaving party on the quay.

Spirit of Portsmouth makes her way elegantly out to Portsmouth Harbour and round to the coastguard station. The chief, Commander Mike Pendleton and his crew escorts the adventurers out to the start line. At about 1150 a maroon goes up, and the crew think it is for them, but the big coastguard cutter which is to escort them out opens up her throttle and churns out of the harbour at 30 knots; a boat is sinking somewhere out in the Gulf of Maine.

Three other boats come to escort them out. Making their way to the lighthouse, the actual starting point for the official timing, the Coastguard are still joking about escorting them off US territory. Soon there are 30 or 40 boats surrounding them, and twelve noon is about to strike. Months of planning have come down to this one moment. Noon.

A gun fires. Alan opens the throttle. The Coastguard wave goodbye long before international waters, and the other boats turn back one by one.

Suddenly *Spirit of Portsmouth* is alone. Destination: Cape Sable, on the southern tip of Nova Scotia, 230 miles away.

Over the past few days, there has been little time to think, and during the first 10 minutes into the trip, they settle quickly back into a familiar routine. This was what they came for. By the end of the first 10 minutes they are four sailors again. And Jan is asleep.

For three hours, the sea is slight, but the wind is expected to increase to force 5, and the temperature is rapidly going down. Alan drives, Steve watches. Vic is very quiet. The land slowly sinks out of sight to the westward.

At 1500, there is a stop for comfort break, a Mars bar, a drink, and a change of drivers. Alan has to wake Jan. The sea is reasonable, and the boat has been handling well, but they are all convinced they can smell diesel. There is a small amount of black smoke coming out of the exhaust which no one can explain, and because the fumes are blowing into the sleeping compartment, they put it down to a following wind.

They set off again. An hour later, Vic is ill. The smell of diesel and exhaust (raw diesel and salt water is horrible) does not help, and neither does the sea, starting to build up to probably a 3 or 4 metre following sea. It reminded Alan that he had been told Vic needed 3000 calories a day to sustain his bodily functions (the others only needed 1600-1800) because he was carrying twice the bodyweight of the others. They had known that it was a potential problem, but if Vic cannot keep food down, there is cause for concern, even this early. Though, to be fair, Alan and Steve feel queasy, too.

The smell of diesel is worrying and no one knows where it is coming from. At 1800 Alan takes over driving, but they pause as a dark and frightening storm crosses their path a few miles ahead. They hear thunder. Sometimes in this area several storms can meet in the same place and it is best to avoid them. In 1991, a swordfish fleet came to grief at almost this very spot in 100 foot waves and 120 mph winds.

The following sea is coming from the starboard quarter but it is still relatively calm. Ahead they can see reverse breaking waves, and very low cloud and rain. They have tea and remember the doughnuts they have brought with them. Alan doesn't like them. When the seagulls don't like them either, they realise that the doughnuts have been subjected to very high temperatures for more than 24 hours and are well and truly off.

The storm only takes about 15 to 20 minutes to pass, and and does not cause them problems, but Vic vomits everything he has eaten and drunk, including the seasickness pill. He is unsteady on his feet and beginning to be slightly irrational, unable to find the comfort zip in his dry suit. He accuses Alan of giving him a faulty suit, at which point the others are surprised to discover he has not tried it on before today.

They are in a typical North Atlantic current, with the following seas continuing. At 2100, Jan takes over driving, and Vic is still being very ill. There is still a strong smell of diesel, but the engine is running perfectly in the big seas. Darkness falls but is still easy to pick their way through the waves.

Day 2 : Monday, June 23

Jan drives on through the night and at 0100 the coast of Nova Scotia is in sight. They have seen their first whale, but now fog is beginning to form, so as they are making good time, they shut the boat down and go to sleep for an hour; Vic cannot keep his watch, Steve is asleep, and the boat needs a driver and a watchkeeper continuously. The rota is not working.

They wake at 0300. The fog is thick now, and it is getting colder. They are soon off Cape Sable.

The strong smell of diesel is still evident, alarmingly; from the computerised fuel gauge system, it appears they are using more fuel than they should be, and it is a major concern. Although they have run the boat this heavy, or close to it, before, they think at that point they may have overloaded it, and it had actually become inefficient. Although it is performing, they are having to drive the boat harder. It is something they will keep a close watch on. At 0400, Jan takes over and drives until 0900.

Steve's job on the fuel is a watching one. A row of lights tells you when you're getting to the bottom of the tank, and when the light flashes you start pumping fuel again from another tank. But Steve is doing most of the watches, as Vic is unable; he is still being sick.

Through the night and the day, the seas have moderated to nearly calm and the boat is running well. They are settling into a rhythm, stopping every 3 hours for snacks. 1400, Jan is driving again, and they approach a large tanker, the first ship they have seen. The ship has no markings, and does not acknowledge them; it passes close by, and instantly *Spirit of Portsmouth* loses all her GPS connections. And the radar. They take photographs of the ship, but it is not likely to do any good. With no electronic guidance, they are down to hand-held compasses.

The crew later find out that there are military exercises in the area, and they (the military) have probably 'cooked' the antennas — a simple matter for them with sophisticated equipment to turn up the boost on their radar which just wipes out the antenna system on the boat. Even later the crew find out that they should have warned the ship of their proximity, but no one has told them. They are still learning.

There are eight or nine hours, some 200 miles, to go to Sydney. They are not worried about navigation at sea with compasses, but the GPS is of most use in finding harbours, especially harbours new to the crew. They still have the little hand-held GPS, which is fortunate.

At the next stop, a large shark, its fin about 10 inches out of the water, circles the boat, curious about the intruder. They move on.

Jan drives until 1800, when Alan takes over. The weather is turning unpleasant as they turn north westwards round the point towards Sydney and the wind against the tide makes the going uncomfortable. It is very cold, and it seems a million miles from Portsmouth. A 50° drop is considerable in little over 24 hours. They are not that much farther north, but they are approaching the Labrador current, a massive body of cold water coming down the west side of Greenland from the frozen Arctic.

The sea is rough, with waves building to 30 feet. They are down to 15 knots for the last 15-18 miles, and picking their way through thousands upon thousands of lobster pots. It is a stressful job to navigate through them; they are so close together that Steve comments that you could walk across them, and they later find there is a local saying that you would never drown out there.

Pilotage into Sydney is made easier by observing a large container ship, and as they are congratulating themselves on their initiative, the propeller picks up a lobster pot line. There is no choice. Alan has to hang in the water over the back of the boat, Steve holding his feet, his mind on the shark they saw not so far back. It is like some sort of naval punishment from Nelson's day. Steve watches Alan trying to cut the line, but he cannot; it has to be carefully unwound. The two minutes seems like an hour, and Alan comes back exhausted, but grateful they had cut the engine quickly — nylon can do as much damage as steel, because it frays, and the fibres get inside the shaft, damaging the oil seal, then you have transmission failure.

There is a strong wind from the north and it is now raining. It has taken them an exhausting two hours to travel the last 30 miles into Sydney. The big harbour entrance is about 4 miles across, and the only directions they have say "Make your way up to the Northern Yacht Club and park outside." They had asked — where's the yacht club? Down on the right hand side. They had left it at that, not knowing that Sydney is a bigger harbour than Portsmouth, and is in fact two harbours.

They drive the boat into what seems like someone's garden — a large berth blown out of the rock below the house on the hillside. There are people getting their fishing boat ready and are happy to point out the yacht club, and the crew are met at the harbour wall by Natalie Marsh, Dr Louise McLeod and a few other well-wishers from North Sydney Rotary Club. It is 1915 Canadian time, 2015 US time, and probably 2315 BST. Jan alters his watch immediately. They are already becoming confused by time zones, but haven't seen anything yet.

For Leg One, they have travelled 658 nautical miles in 31.25 hours, and used 750 litres of fuel, leaving 250 litres in the tanks, and it is at this point Steve realises they are using nearly one and a quarter litres per nautical mile instead of the expected one litre. There is evidently a leak, and they have travelled 100 miles further than they thought, having had to drive up and down the big Atlantic waves. Fuel estimates will have to be revised. Timing estimates have to be revised, too — they can expect to travel 100 miles in 5 hours from now on, instead of the more optimistic 4.

The superbly hospitable people of N Sydney take the crew to the Clansman Hotel, where they are welcome to negotiate the price of a meal.

Alan telephones his son, James, and Jonathan Smith of The News, back home. Vic feels a great deal better, and tucks into a big T-bone steak. In his case, food now seems to be the key, and sleeping in a bed. They are all relieved to have him back, and turn in for an early night, very tired from the day's battering.

Day 3 : Tuesday, June 24

Sydney, Nova Scotia

The crew wake up feeling very much refreshed, including Vic, and Natalie Marsh and her partner Harry King show them round the town. North Sydney is a small, bleak and isolated fishing and coal mining community, and reminds Alan of TV's Northern Exposure; he expects to see a moose walking down the street. Although the capital city of Nova Scotia, it is dying on its feet, as are many other places.

When the boat is lifted out of the water at the yacht club, Alan and Vic are determined to find the cause of the diesel smell. It comes to Alan quite suddenly when he remembers that on the previous Thursday, Joe Poulter from Yamaha had called him so say he should make a slight modification to the engine. With all the other preparations, Alan had forgotten about it. A little rubber pipe over the turbo lift pump is sited wrongly, and water is getting trapped in it. Alan removes the turbo pump and clears the water out. It is as simple as that.

Vic turns his attention to the radar. It has obviously stopped working because, he says, it has been 'zapped'. He quickly becomes a radar specialist as he takes it apart. Soon it is working again. Alan changes the GPS antennas and soon they are working again, too. Meanwhile, Steve and Jan have been shopping for the next leg's provisions. Alan and Vic's next job is to further inflate the tubes for the colder waters when they go north. Temperatures are expected to drop to freezing point. An inspection of the hull reveals that they must have hit something in the night, because there is a large piece missing, so that is quickly repaired. It has been a hard day's work maintaining the boat, only to be expected with a relatively new boat and the first long leg, but there has still been time for drinks during the day at the yacht club and some relaxing chats with the locals.

In the evening they are entertained by the Rotary Club and well-wishers with a traditional fish and chip supper, including fish soup, at Natalie's parents' house. The drink, and the conversation, flows freely.

FOURTEEN : LEG TWO

Nova Scotia to Labrador

Day 4 : Wednesday, June 25

The plan is to leave Sydney this evening — but only if the wind changes from the north. If they do, it means any ice they encounter on the way to Labrador will be during the day time, rather than in the dark. In some ways they are reluctant to be leaving — what they have seen, they have liked enormously, and Alan promises to return with his family.

A Cape Breton Regional Gazette journalist asks: "Alan Priddy and Vic Palmer are engineers by trade; Steve Lloyd is a floor layer and Jan Falkowski is a psychiatrist. So, are these men insane?"

Alan has the answer: "Not according to our doctor."

They have had another good night's sleep, and Vic is his usual, laughing self. It is an easy day, with time for a look round. They have made arrangements for a fuel tanker to come down at midday, when they take 750 litres of fuel on board.

Natalie's brother is in the coastguard, and is keeping them up to date with the weather forecast. It s from this point that they will start getting ice forecasts, because the ice is coming further south this year than usual. The forecast is explicit, and even tells how many icebergs they are likely to encounter; one forecast estimates 40 icebergs an hour in the Labrador current. The crew did not expect to have to deal with ice after just 650 miles.

Taking local advice during lunch, the decision is taken to leave at dusk. The local epithet runs: "The wind goes down with the sun and comes up with the sun."

The advice is accurate — at 1800, just before sunset, they say goodbye to their new friends at Sydney and within an hour it is flat calm. Alan drives until 2300, when Jan takes over, and it is still completely flat calm. Alan and Steve are able to sleep, but have taken the precaution of seasickness pills. The are under no illusions; the sea will not be flat calm all the way to Labrador.

The evening is dark, but bright with stars, and they enjoy them in the knowledge that they will not see darkness again until they reach Northern Ireland.

And that is a long way ahead.

Day 5 : Thursday, June 26

Gulf of St Lawrence and Belle Isle Strait

At 0300 Alan takes over the wheel from Jan. The time disorientation is already taking effect — when he is woken, he cannot believe the time, because it is broad daylight. Their watches come to mean less and less as they proceed, still in the flat calm waters of the Belle Isle Strait between Newfoundland and Quebec. They change drivers again after three hours and, at 0605, Steve points to something in the distance. It is their first iceberg.

When it snows in Greenland, which it does most of the time, each fall of snow is compacted by the last. After a few thousand years, the incredibly dense ice produced as a result creeps its way down the glaciers a few inches a year and eventually reaches the sea, where pieces break off and float slowly southwards in the Labrador current. This piece is the size of a single storey house, and it wallows benignly in their path.

Steve notes their position as 51°18'N, 57°01'W as they drive slowly towards the berg. Totally amazed, the crew forget all the advice they have been given (to leave it alone), and go up to it like children with a new toy. It is pure white, with a smooth surface where the outside is melting; below the water it is an opaque turquoise of the quality of the jewel. They drive around it, and touch it. The melt water is dripping from it in quantity. Someone has the idea to plant the flag of Portsmouth on it, so they go round to its lee side and move in close, crab-wise as the berg is moving up and down in the water about 6 metres.

In a movement worthy of Captain Ahab, Vic lunges at it with the flagstaff. It bounces off. Seconds later, there is a roar from within like that from an injured animal, and the berg tips away from them, bring up a surge of water underneath the boat. Alan rapidly jabs the throttle open and they rush clear. 20 metres or so away, they break out a snack, and minutes later there is another crash and the berg splits in half. Now the two icebergs have to find their equilibrium again, and roll about, eventually capsizing.

The crew smile reassuringly at each other — they are thinking: ice — easy; floating bungalows, no problem.

From then on, there are many icebergs, all less friendly, and most bigger. They are the size of blocks of flats now, and the sea is no longer calm. Whales are becoming so familiar they are hardly noticed as they steer clear of the boat which they will have heard coming many miles away. Humpbacks and sperm whales are easy to identify, and there are several other species, including pilot whales and dolphins. Most of the whales are considerably bigger than the boat.

They are back out into the Atlantic now, heading towards Battle Harbour, and the weather is awful. Vic is unwell again — his sense of humour has gone. The seas are confused, reminding them of Alderney Race, only 10 times worse. It is early evening and Vic, who has been navigating, and had on the first trip to the USA with Alan chosen all the charts, is expected to guide them in. With the rocks looming closer in the crashing seas, Alan passes him the map, and asks where they are but Vic throws it back at him angrily and says he doesn't know. They realise later this is a symptom of his sickness, but right now there is no time to argue, and Jan and Steve between them pick out the headlands they need. The wind is against the tide, the huge following seas are breaking, and Alan needs all his skill to get the boat through. There is only one mistake, and it is almost a disaster — they are looking for two conspicuous towers, Steve shouts that he can see them, and Alan looks away and the boat dives straight into the back of a wave. Freezing water fills the boat, crashing over them.

Within about three minutes, the water is out and they are recovering from their shock submergence. The seas are worsening rapidly, and ice is everywhere. The stress is not knowing how deep it is, or where the submerged rocks are, and there is little time for discussion as they plunge into the little harbour. Vic soberly shakes all their hands, and says they have done well. He does not look well.

They can breathe again, and again that look goes between them. They have done the ice. Not so easy this time, but they have done it. Noting in the log that the ice is further south than it should be at that time of year, they tie up in what seems a deserted and barren Battle Harbour at 1410, Canadian time. It has taken them 20 hours and 10 minutes to travel the 509 miles from Sydney, a good run averaging 28 knots. Fuel consumption was the same — 1.25 litres per nautical mile. They have done the ice, and the bad seas; it can only get better.

FIFTEEN : LEG THREE

Labrador to Greenland

If all you knew about Labrador was that a dog was named after it, you may be surprised.

Anyone wanting to get a feel for the place as it was a few years ago should read Hammond Innes's novel *The Land God Gave To Cain*, which gives some idea of the desolation of the place, but it is possible to scrape up a few facts about the region from here and there.

Labrador is not a province of Canada, as some people mistakenly think, but the name given to part of the large peninsula between Ungava Bay and the Belle Isle Strait in the north east of Canada, with a coastline in the Davis Strait and North Atlantic. Part lies in Quebec and part in Newfoundland.

It is an area rich in potential resources, including minerals, power, forestry and fishing. Conditions, however, make exploitation difficult — it's northerly situation means harsh winters and short summers.

Formerly more industrial than today, some areas are undergoing a revival with the advent of more modern technology and dwindling resources elsewhere.

Day 5 : Thursday, June 26 (continued)

Battle Harbour

More than a year before his arrival in Battle Harbour, Alan received a letter from this remote place as a result of making inquiries about refuelling stops.

Alan was delighted. Along with the letter was some information on Battle Harbour, which is fascinating enough to repeat here in full. Although, when you have read it, you may notice an intriguing contrast between what the tired and battered crew found, and what they were led to expect.

                    Battle Harbour Historic Trust
       Station "A", Happy Valley — Goose Bay, Labrador A0P 1S0

                                                        March 8, 1996

Rotarian Alan Priddy
Hayling Island,
Hampshire, England

Dear Alan,
       Your cry for help regarding a suitable stopover in
Labrador has been heard. Your suggestion of Battle Harbour as
a potential layover point is a good one and I think I can be of
assistance in making the necessary arrangements. I'll explain.
       On the day that your letter arrived in Labrador I
happened to be chairing our weekly Rotary luncheon meeting. As
a result it fell to me to read and act upon your request. You
can imagine my surprise as I read your letter since, when I'm
not at Rotary, I'm the Project Manager for the Battle Harbour
Historic Trust. I'll enclose a blurb about the Trust and its
objectives but, in short, we are engaged in restoring about
twenty historic structures at Battle Harbour, the most
historically significant community on Labrador's south coast.
The project is scheduled for official completion in 1997, and a
number of special events will be planned around the site's
opening ceremonies — it may be that your visit will coincide
with some of these. In any case, I'm certain that you will
find the community both interesting and capable of providing
the necessary amenities and supplies for your voyage. Diesel
fuel will not be a problem and the on-site shop carries a good
selection of foodstuffs, etc. In the event that there are
requirements that can't be provided at Battle Harbour there are
three nearby communities (each about ten miles from Battle
Harbour) which should be able to accommodate your needs. Fax
and telephone facilities are available and Coastguard in Goose
Bay will be able to give you updates on existing ice edge and
forecasts of ice movements, as well as file your sail plan.
       I suggest that as the time draws closer you let me know
details of your visit, when you'll arrive, the number in your
party, length of stay, etc. I'll be glad to help out. If you
wish you can contact me directly at telephone. 709 497 8805 or
fax 709 497 8807 until June after which I'll be in Battle
Harbour at telephone./fax 709 921 6216.
                            Sincerely,

                            Tom Paddon
                          Project Manager

BATTLE HARBOUR HISTORY

The mercantile salt fish premises at Battle Harbour were established by the firm of John Slade & Co of Poole, England between 1750 and 1775. Lying just north of the old French Shore, Battle Harbour served as the gateway for Newfoundlanders seeking to fish unmolested in the resource rich waters of Labrador. Its location led to the Slade premises becoming the major base for the region's cod and seal fisheries and for the commercial trade that led to the formation of a permanent community.

The local population increased rapidly after 1830 when Newfoundland fishing schooners adopted Battle Harbour as their primary port of call and made it the recognized capital of the Labrador floater fishery. Battle Harbour remained in the hands of Slade until 1871, and during this time became a settled community, dominated by the fish merchants, but with its own evolving institutions, especially schools and churches. In 1871 the Slades sold Battle Harbour to Baine, Johnston & Co who operated the site in much the same manner until 1955. The activity of these two firms at Battle Harbour is an accurate microcosm of the history of Newfoundland and Labrador's fishery over almost two centuries. Community development here was unparalleled along the Labrador coast, and became the *de facto* regional capital with the requisite legal, religious, educational and health facilities. Noted ecclesiastical architect William Gray, under the direction of Bishop Edward Field, designed the church of St James the Apostle in the late 1840s. Built in 1852 and restored in 1991, it is the sole surviving example of Gray's work. It is also the second oldest wooden Anglican church in Newfoundland.

In the years of Baine, Johnston & Co, activity at Battle Harbour attracted the interest of the Royal National Mission to Deep Sea Fishermen (later to become the International Grenfell Association). Dr Wilfred Grenfell arrived in Battle Harbour in 1892 and a year later built his first hospital in the community. It was also Newfoundland's first hospital outside of St John's. Further institutions attracted to Battle Harbour as the region's natural centre of operations included the Canadian Marconi Company, the Newfoundland Ranger Force — who chose it as the location of their first Labrador detachment — and later, after Confederation, the Royal Canadian Mounted Police.

The community's amenities and communications services also lent themselves to the role of 'jump off' point for the polar explorers. Commander Robert E Peary was a familiar figure in Battle Harbour and it was there that in 1909 he wired his account of reaching the Pole to the outside world. It was also the site of the press conference, attended by news correspondents from as far away as New York, that was instrumental in touching off the great controversy between Peary and Cook as to who exactly had reached the Pole first, if at all. The controversy occupied the front page of the New York Times for ten days and is still under debate in the 1990s.

In 1955 Baine, Johnston & Co sold the premises to the Earle Brothers Freighting Services who continued the site's operations until the decline of the inshore fishery at the start of the 1990s. At that time the site was turned over to the Historic Trust. The community's permanent residents had been relocated under a government sponsored resettlement program in 1968, although a number of families still use the site as a seasonal summer home.

Alan and his crew step ashore to what they can only describe as an odd and troubling atmosphere. The place reeks, not of fish as it once would have done, but of history. They each have different impressions, and most of them are mediaeval, reminiscent of burning at the stake, although the place is not old enough to carry such ghostly impressions.

The language is odd. It is a little while before you realise it is English. The fact there are no Ts or Hs disguises it totally. There are so many Ts and Hs in the language that if you miss them all out it sounds as if you are using only vowels. The crew have not felt like foreigners anywhere more than here.

They have their own time zone, which is 35 minutes less than Eastern time, or 3 hours 25 minutes different from Greenwich Mean Time.

There are a number of historic buildings which are being renovated, and some non-historic buildings which need renovating. There is a general store that does not really sell anything. There is an inn which serves food like pea soup with something like semolina floating on the top It tastes neither of peas nor semolina. They cannot stay at the inn because it has been fully booked by a film crew, whose helicopter is outside.

The crew introduce themselves to Keith Poole, Project Manager of Battle Harbour, a pleasant man in charge of spending 4 million Canadian dollars restoring the site. He is welcoming. They are escorted by his business manager, a girl they think is called Ina House, though with the local pronunciation they cannot be sure, to a rustic bunkhouse which is to be their billet for the duration of their stay. When they get there, they are hot from walking in the sun in thermal gear, and she tells them: "Whatever you do, don't let the wood stove go out." In the hut there are two stoves, one in the living quarters, and one in the kitchen, providing hot water and for cooking. There are about 8 beds, some with mattresses, some without. There are a few thin, poor sleeping bags, but the crew, already accustomed to sleeping in the bottom of a boat, do not mind. They are dead tired. The place is as quiet as the grave. Associations form in tired minds, and they find themselves checking whether there are locks on the doors. There are not. They have already been told that a Belgian sailor has arrived that morning after sailing from Australia. The crew haven't seen him. Nor a boat in the harbour. The film 'The Wicker Man' is mentioned. And 'Deliverance'. They realise they are in one of the most remote communities in the world; they turn in, wearily, Jan with his commando knife on in case he has to fight his way out — they are not going to burn <u>him</u>. No one has loaded the wood stove. No one has thought of it because they are too hot already; Alan even changes bunk so he can sleep by an open window. It is not long before they are awake, frozen. The temperature has gone down to -10° and it is unbelievably cold.

Day 6 : Friday, June 27

Battle Harbour

When the crew rise next morning, despite being very cold, it is pouring with rain. They cannot start the fire — even with their underpants, which are generally discarded each day. They try to imagine what the place is like in winter, but cannot. They go instead to Keith's office, which has the only telephone on the site. Alan speaks to Per Neilson in Greenland who has the bad news that the ice is solid, but may shift later, perhaps Sunday or Monday.

Checking the boat over, they find nothing wrong. It is still pouring with rain, and there is absolutely nothing to do, so they set out for a walk round the island, which they discover is about 3 by 2 miles. It will be a short walk, punctuated only by planting a flag on the highest point. Even this, they are later told, will be washed by the spray from the huge seas that batter the island in the worst storms.

Soon a gale is blowing. There is a great deal of ice in the harbour, which should not be there at this time of year. Calling at the inn, they discover the film crew is from Canadian Geographic, there to shoot a multi-million dollar film re-enacting an expedition of a famous Antarctic explorer. When Alan comments that this is the Arctic, he is told it is cheaper than the real thing. Oh yes, and not so cold. The penguins will be imported for the picture — if there are penguins, people will believe it. The star is to be Mel Gibson. Alan muses that if Canadian Geographic were spending that sort of money, perhaps he should have contacted them… The film crew are shown *Spirit of Portsmouth* and are amazed.

Deciding that a good place to look at the history of any place is the graveyard, they head for it, taking in the reservoir on the way. The graveyard is high on a hill, and in the middle of it, a coffin, held down with rocks. They look round for Vic, who has disappeared momentarily, and Jan points at the coffin, lightening the tension, but only just. When they get back to the inn (Vic having reappeared), they ask about the coffin, and everyone shrugs their shoulders as if to say: What coffin? Later, while Alan is telling Keith about this, the latter is sketching a picture of Alan; it is quite good, but then he notices Keith has drawn a fish hook in the corner of the mouth. Jan is most interested to hear about it.

A strange thing happens in Battle Harbour on Fridays; everybody leaves. The population goes down to 4: someone who can only be described as a lunatic, his wife, Ina and Keith Poole. During the week the population is 28. The crew is now half the population.

Western Atlantic: Whale sightings are frequent

Belle Isle Strait: The first iceberg

Labrador: The last dawn for two weeks

Approaching Battle Harbour: a hint of things to come

Battle Harbour

Battle Harbour: The highest point

Greenland: The Agdlek finally breaks through the pack

Greenland: On board Agdlek as she attempts to fight her way back to the coast

Keith goes to the mainland, St Mary's Harbour, to get some beer, because the crew think it is the only way they will get through another evening. They wait for the fuel barge. Eventually, a rusty old hulk comes chugging into the harbour, and in a very strange accent its skipper says *"U R wan ur full?"* Alan, getting used to the language, answers: "Yes, please, we want some fuel." *"Ow er u wan?"* "About 800 litres, please."

He is soon filling the boat with fuel, standing over them, staring impassively. Alan asks, does he know what the weather is going to be like tomorrow? *"Wer, don' concern myself with weather. Pree much same as day before round ere."* Alan asks, does he listen to it on the radio? *"No ime lis'en er radio."* They get no more out of him, and once more Alan hears duelling banjos.

They take on 600 litres — and find the diesel leak; it is in the corner of one of the tanks. As it is not patchable, Steve makes a note to run that tank dry first, and thus minimise the loss. Keith Poole has not returned, so they return to the bunkhouse, keep the stove going, and wait for ice and weather reports.

The one telephone on the island, which only works intermittently when someone remembers to operate the generator, does not have a fax facility, and weather fax reports have to come from the mainland by dinghy. Later that evening, an ice report arrives, along with Keith who, for ease of carrying, has the beers inside him and is not a great deal of help in translating the Danish ice patrol's reports. The upshot is that, although the ice report suggests Greenland is going to be difficult, it is not apparent to the novice Arctic sailor. The situation is that the wind has come down from the Arctic from two directions, and the two flows meet at Cape Farewell, forming solid ice in that region. Alan has earlier telephoned Greenland, who have said that if they get there just as the tide is going out, there should be a passage into Nanortalik. And since the ice report says nine tenths ice, forever the optimists the crew decide to go. They have a tenth to play with, after all…

```
fax from Per Neilson
Friday 29 June, 1600 BST

Ice very bad in Nanortalik at present.
Unlikely to improve until southerly winds change to north west.
Control at base will send you XES now and in 4 hours.  At
present they state 8 tenths to 9 tenths cover off coast in
region of Nanortalik.
Good luck — be very careful.  Love from the girls
```

They do not know that nine tenths ice means impassable. There might be an ice field measuring 30 miles by 10, and it might have a hole in the middle 500 yards round. In other words, the one tenth water could be in the middle. And the ice referred to is broken ice which the tide has pushed together outside of the 30 by 10 of solid ice. But, without anyone to ask for advice, they believe they can get a small boat through.

Day 7 : Saturday, June 28

Leaving Battle Harbour

This is their last chance to opt for a direct route to Iceland, but after much discussion and more faxes, they agree they will try to get to Greenland. The ice reports say the field is moving, and if they arrive as the tide is going out they should be able to make a landfall between the ice. It sounds easy. In principle.

As Battle Harbour is the only place on land or sea throughout the whole trip that they have been concerned, they are not sorry to leave, which they do at 12.20 local (Goose Bay) time, which is Eastern less 35 minutes, which is 3 hours 25 minutes behind BST. Probably.

They all feel fit and rested. Alan drives out into a completely flat sea. They clear the rocks with no difficulty and set a course north east for Nanortalik, full of optimism and enthusiasm to explore Greenland, despite the steady rain. Jan takes over after three and a half hours. At 1700 they come against a wall of fog, and are relying totally on the Raytheon radar. Visibility is nil. It is suddenly very cold. Alan takes over at 1900; it is still very foggy and cold, and soon the sea is being roughed up by a force 6 from the north. But instead of blowing away the fog, it becomes thicker, and is freezing. It penetrates their eyes, noses and ears. It is horrible.

The fog is not blowing away for a simple reason. There are 400 miles of it, and they drive steadily on, hour after hour. It is still raining, and it is freezing as it falls, and Jan drives from 2200 while the others try to shelter from it.

They have started getting salt burns and salt pops. The sea water gets inside gloves and swells up the skin. Throughout the trip it gets worse. They will carry the scars for weeks, and if the hands swell up too much the blisters have to be lanced. But the crew are amazed what discomfort they can put with; not that there is any choice. Alan recalls later — you can accommodate the level of pain and it just becomes part of you. You notice it at times, like when you have to stretch your dry suit over your hands; it does not improve while you are on stopovers — there isn't time — but you notice the pain more than when you are at sea, when you are more active.

Day 8 : Sunday, June 29

Davis Strait

Alan takes over from Jan at 0320. The conditions have not changed. At 0700, Jan has taken over again and it is still foggy, but the rain has stopped at last and the sea is moderating. They cannot keep their hands warm, even in their pockets, and their feet are the same. Coming off watch, they lie in the bottom of the boat trying to rest, but not sleeping because there is a semi-conscious urge to keep toes and fingers moving to keep the blood flowing — frostbite is in all their minds. But there is no ice, and they are full of optimism

They are changing drivers every two hours now to stave off boredom and help concentration. The radar is working well, even in the rough sea. But Vic is showing signs of deteriorating again.

By 1900, they are probably no more than 12 miles from Nanortalik, and the atmosphere suddenly changes. It is quieter, and there is a strange smell. Then there are different sounds, slapping, unearthly sounds, eerie in the light fog. They slow down, and there in front of them is a solid wall of ice, about 4 feet high. The fog is clearing as they deviate to find a safe passage through, and they realise, however far they look, it stretches to the horizon in either direction. Nanortalik is iced in.

The ice is moving, with icebergs locked in it, and there are no leads visible. It is -10° and raining again. They go back into clear water for a while to gather themselves, remembering what they have been told.

The International Ice Patrol survey continuously. Since it was set up shortly after the *Titanic* disaster, no ships outside the "limit of all known ice" have hit any. Three times a week, 8 hours a day, during the March to July season, patrols are constant, using a combination of radar and visual searching. The Patrol also predicts the flow of the Labrador current (which carrie the ice southwards) by dropping buoys, indicating speed and direction.

Ice comes in various forms. Sea ice is formed and broken up by current weather, whereas icebergs are more dense and have come from glaciers. Sea ice is predictable; icebergs are not — the amount below the water can be as little as 70% and as much as 90%, depending on the density of the ice and the salt content. Some icebergs weigh as much as a ton per cubic yard, and rollers (where the ice under the water is melting quickly and at some point will result in the iceberg inverting) are the most dangerous. But while the crew know all this, it does not help them get to Nanortalik. And the ice is moving towards them with the tide.

Not only is the ice moving, it is also rolling in the swell. That is the slapping sound. They did not realise how it grew; there is an iceberg the size of a house, which meets three or four smaller 'bergs the size of cars, and in an instant the house has become a block of flats; they have stuck together, and the continual movement is opening up small gaps and closing them again. They now see what nine tenths ice is.

There is no way in, at least not very far; at first they are sure that, as a small boat, there will be a passage somewhere, and they are crabbing across the tide, but the leads are closing behind them. It becomes clear that they are going to be caught, crushed even. There are openings, but not necessarily near enough to reach before they close again. Eventually, they are in a small lake, surrounded by ice, they can no longer see the sea, and the lake is shrinking. Alan drives the boat up on to the lowest part of the ice, hoping it will break. It does, and they breathe a sigh of relief as they reach the open sea again.

They try several times to get in when a lead opens up, but soon realise they are closing as quickly as they open. A big lump of ice hits the gearbox, overloading the power trim on it and the leg comes out of the water just as they need forward speed. The leg will not go back down, so Alan quickly manually overrides it while Jan drives.

The frustrating thing is that, as they continue to look for a passage through the ice, they can now see the stretch of coastline on which Nanortalik lies. There is clearly no option but to wait, but even that hope is disappearing rapidly as they realise they are being pushed southwards at 2.5 knots by the ice, which is moving with the tide.

Alan contacts the Greenland Coastguard by radio. He is very surprised when they answer quite quickly and clearly in English. He explains the situation. The response: what the hell are you doing out there? Ice patrol stations in Greenland have been warning that only icebreakers should attempt to put to sea. Alan points out they are not asking for help, but advice. There is a twenty minute delay; it seems like an hour. The radio crackles, and the advice is to go 120 miles north up the Davis Strait, where Arsuk Harbour should be open.

It is the last thing they need to do. Alan questions it, in view of their proximity to Nanortalik; he explains it will take up all fuel reserves and could they assure him he will get into Arsuk? They confirm.

It is a painful decision; every mile they go north is another mile on the next leg to Iceland. Once it is evident they are not going to get to

Nanortalik, the crew put on warmer clothing. It is now severely below freezing, and the rain is turning into balls of ice as it hits the sea. They realise they have not understood ice at all as they clear away offshore again, among the floating icebergs and begin to pick their way north.

The thick ice is easy enough to avoid; despite the freezing rain, visibility is reasonable. Some of the smaller floes bounce off the boat. It is a painful process, and a steep learning curve — white ice is visible, but there is black ice, too, the transparent blocks of metal-hard ice which floats just beneath the water. Whoever's hand is on the throttle when black ice hits the boat has to shut it off before the ice contacts the propeller. Alan, confident in Jan's driving, tries to sleep in the bow. The absence of darkness is confusing, but it is now night.

Day 9 : Monday, June 30

Pack Ice off Greenland

Mile after mile, banging and scraping. Alan is resting, jarred painfully awake by each thud on the hull, and eventually his head appears: "For God's sake, go south and clear this lot."

Jan and Steve chorus: "Go back to sleep, Alan." They have been doing just that for two hours. Eventually there is less ice, and they cover the 120 miles to the area off Arsuk, using the radar, GPS and the sight lines thoughtfully provided on the chart, which probably date from the 1920s. But it is just as it was off Nanortalik — the coast is locked in, and they cannot get within 10 miles of the shore. It is a sickening thought that they have travelled those 120 miles for nothing and that they are no better off.

It is 0300. They have a conference. We're here; let's find a way in. But it is even heavier than off Nanortalik. Alan takes over the wheel, and Jan sleeps, but Steve stays on watch as they try, again and again, to find a lead into the pack. Vic is unable to take a watch. There is no respite, not a single moment to stop and take stock. They cannot eat or drink. Some of the icebergs are immense, the size of department stores, and they are all moving at 3 knots, but not necessarily in the same direction, and between them the sea ice is forming and reforming; the noise is deafening. They go offshore again and wake Jan. It is time for another conference.

There are two aspects to consider. First, fuel is low, as they have used their reserves getting to Arsuk; they have to keep motoring to charge the batteries and prevent the fuel from freezing; they have to keep moving anyway — when they stop, the sea freezes around the boat. Second, if they call for help they are more likely to be rescued by helicopter than a ship, which effectively means abandoning the boat. Alan confides to Steve he fears they have a total loss on their hands — they have not been able to insure the boat outside of British territorial waters.

It is -20° now, still raining, and the wind is increasing; the wind chill factor could be as low as -40°. Their hands are a mass of white, pussy skin, and their faces are burning in the wind. At these temperatures, the gas stove has given up and it is too cold for the alcohol stove. It is no surprise to see on the chart that they have just passed Cape Desolation. They agree to ask for further advice, and radio the Greenland Coastguard again. There is no answer. Alan puts out a call to any station. 20 minutes pass before an answer comes through. It seems forever, although they know there will be a response — back in 1930 there was a major shipping incident off Greenland and the Danes were found wanting, so they now are now assiduous in maintaining a search and rescue facility for the whole of Greenland.

Alan is soon explaining their situation. The coastguard are amazed. *"You should not be here."* Alan refrains from the language he might have used in different circumstances. He tells them: "You sent us here. Now what? We do not have enough fuel to go anywhere else. We're not in danger, but we're cold. What do you suggest?" *"Wait."* They wait. Ten minutes later they have their answer: *"The Danish Navy will be out to pick you up. Out."* There is no chance to ask: Who? Us or the boat? It is a strange, out-worldly experience to sit quietly in the Arctic, despite the engine idling comfortingly, not knowing what the immediate future will bring. The sea slaps sluggishly, and there is no sign of life anywhere outside the boat. It is colder than they have ever known, and Jan believes Vic is not only suffering badly from exhaustion, but is in the early stages of hypothermia. 2 hours pass. The radio makes them jump. It is the captain of the *R.D.N.S. Agdlek*, a Royal Danish Navy vessel, asking for their position. Alan tells him and includes their rate of drift, and the captain says he will be there in about four hours. He is 15 miles away.

While the four hours pass — slowly — the crew have several conversations with the captain of the *Agdlek*, who is pleasantly surprised that three of the crew at least are not hypothermic and in reasonably good shape, and it is with considerable relief to the crew that at last they see the ship's lights in the pale grey distance. The final call is the captain explaining he will be longer; the ice is just passable, but with difficulty. Alan replies that he will come in as close as he can. It is another hour before the *Agdlek* clears the ice pack and *Spirit of Portsmouth* manoeuvres on to her starboard side.

The *Agdlek* is not strictly an icebreaker, but a frigate capable of moving through three metres' thickness of ice. Two lines are thrown over, and the adventurers climb aboard, still uncertain whether they are stepping off their RIB for the last time. It is with considerable relief that they hear the captain say he sees no reason for them to abandon the boat. Over a cup of coffee they learn that they were expected to be in a very bad way, and the hospital has been put on alert. The captain and crew could not be more pleasant.

The captain has to plot a new course back to base, because the way they had come out was becoming impassable already. He also announces his intention of towing *Spirit of Portsmouth* behind them, but will not be responsible for any damage. Alan is grateful for small mercies, and watches as the crew attach a 15 metre line to the RIB. They go to the mess and the captain treats them to lunch while they swap tales of the sea in a congenial and warm, but somehow unreal atmosphere. Afterwards, Alan and Steve take a nap while Jan goes out to film *Spirit of Portsmouth* from the deck of the ship. *Agdlek* is punching through and over the ice, and each piece which breaks off scrapes along the side of the ship and under the transom, where it crashes into the following RIB, or the RIB is simply dragged over it. When he sees the video a little later, Alan is certain the boat will have been wrecked.

During the long and arduous passage back to the ship's base, Alan and the crew are surprised to learn that the ship is attached to, and they are bound for, the Grønlands Kommando, Denmark's commando base in Kangilinnguit, Grønnedal, since Greenland is supposed to be independent. They also learn that the area they are heading for is the only 'green' part of Greenland and that, legend has it, Erik the Red landed here, saying he had found a magical green pasture.

When they steam up the fjord and arrive at the naval base, it is about 1430 — they have been at sea for almost 50 hours, and travelled just 600 miles. In contrast with the welcome on the ship, the base is not so friendly, and the crew are made to feel they are intruding, and even stupid to be there at all. Security is strict; the satellite equipment and flares are confiscated. Alan is permitted to send one fax to say they are safe on land, but they do not allow him to use the telephone.

They are interrogated in a reasonable, but cold manner by a senior officer, and realise that they are not above suspicion as spies. It is an uncomfortable time until they can convince their hosts — or captors — that they are genuine adventurers. Some of the suspicion obviously is based on the fact that *Spirit of Portsmouth* is kitted out professionally and not without a hint of military efficiency.

The crew are finally glad, especially Vic, who is exhausted, to be shown to pleasant rooms in the civilian quarter to get some much needed showers and rest after a very long and stressful day.

Day 10 : Tuesday, July 1

Greenland

The crew are very disappointed not to have got to Nanortalik; they have been intrigued by the brochure they were sent before setting out; however, they determine to make the best of their stay.

Greenland is the world's largest island, yet has a population of only about 50,000 people — Inuit (the indigenous people, formerly known generally as eskimos), Danish and other Europeans. The country is rich in minerals and fish are plentiful around its coasts although, as the crew of *Spirit of Portsmouth* have found, it is subject to very harsh conditions for much of the year. During the Cold War, the island was strategically important. The capital is Nuuk, and there are numerous settlements around the coastline.

The interior is uninhabited, and indeed largely uninhabitable. Following the Vikings' landing there about 1000 years ago, the country remained under the rule of Norway until it was taken over by Denmark about 200 years ago, and then became self-governing in 1981.

When Alan, Jan, Steve and Vic arrive, they learn it has been raining and freezing cold for three weeks. And this is summer. But they awake on the Tuesday morning to a different atmosphere, inside and out. Their reason for being there has been established, and the commandos are curious and friendly. They are shown where to eat, and what there is to do on the base. There is a gym and a games room, for example, and a friendly canteen. Apart from that, there is little to occupy a visitor's time. Alan learns that the Danes have spent a great deal of money restoring a Greenlandic village, but that it is cosmetic — Greenland has not prospered. He gets the impression that with only 6 million people living in Denmark, and with Greenland probably five times the size, they are investing considerable time and money on mineral research, with the ultimate aim of eventual great wealth. Of the minority of civilians, many are construction workers, but little seems to be under construction. Steve believes they are mostly painters and decorators. However, it is their principal base for naval operations.

They are iced in, and there is nothing to do but wait for the weather to change. Although at the end of a fjord, and in pleasant enough surroundings and clement enough weather — there is no snow on the ground, only on the hillsides and mountains — they know that for 15 miles out to sea it is solid ice. It will be hard to wait, knowing that it could be weeks before they can get on with the challenge.

Having got up for breakfast, they go back to bed until midday.

While Jan and Vic play snooker, Steve and Alan go for a walk — it is a relief to be wearing normal clothes — and climb a nearby mountain in deck shoes. It is harder than they think, through ice and rocks, and at a certain height the temperature drops suddenly, but at least it has stopped raining. From the top, they can see how the glaciers come down to the sea and break off to form the icebergs which have been so menacing on the water. They take a drink of pure spring water and head back down again. There is no sign of wildlife — it has been said at the base that "If it moves, someone will kill and eat it." They have seen an eagle, and Alan suspects it may have formed part of their last meal.

In the afternoon, leaving Vic to sleep, Steve, Jan and Alan go to the Greenlandic village, about 5 kilometres away. It is deserted and dismal. As they are walking back, the only Greenlandic person to speak to them is curiously the man who's job it is to make sure the generators run in the village — for nobody to be there. The only English word he speaks is "Hom" (home) and he says it with feeling: "I want to go home." Not considering that the village was worth the effort of the 10 kilometre walk, the group are grateful to accept a lift back to the base.

Vic has started to recover, but spends much of his time eating and sleeping to try to restore his strength, which has deteriorated to the point where he cannot walk far, and certainly not down to the boat. He can just manage the bar at 50 paces away, and the canteen at 100 paces. Steve has an upset stomach, put down to eating raw herring, a staple food in these parts; sometimes they are not sure what they are eating.

Alan uses Jan's hand-held GPS (which has been returned) to work on alternative routes to Iceland, but acknowledges there is a serious problem. If the ice stays, so do they.

They are hoping Vic will continue to improve. It has been touch and go as to whether he can continue, or rather may need a short stay in the hospital. But the easy life at the base is doing him good.

The crew all have a good evening in the bar with the commandos, swapping stories and T-shirts. They are big men — so much so their urinals are too tall for the Englishmen.

They begin to talk about aborting the trip, but if they do, where will they go? Alan declares a preference for returning to America to salvage some of their holiday, and enjoy it in civilisation, at which point Steve has a sense of humour failure: "We're not even going to talk about quitting; we're going on, even if we have to wait to the very limit here. We've got this far. We're going on." No one argues; they know he is right. There is no more talk of giving up.

Day 11 : Wednesday, July 2

Greenland

All the time spent watching the weather reports does not improve their chances of getting away, but in the morning they hear the icebreaker is going fishing, so they ask if it will be possible to lift the RIB out of the water first, which the captain readily agrees to.

The crew are astonished to see, when the boat is raised above the deck and they are able to spin it in the air, that the battering through the ice has not left a single mark on the hull.

The Greenlanders are happy, too, because they do not want the Englishmen to stay indefinitely.

The boat is refuelled and, weather permitting, they are ready to go. It is clear that Nanortalik is no longer a possibility for even a brief visit, about which the crew are sorry, especially as they have not been able to get word there.

It will be a straight run for Iceland, but with the extra 120 miles to do they break out all the spare fuel tanks and fill them, too. When the operation is complete, there are 1300 litres of fuel on board. 5000 kroner, please, say the Danes. Alan feels it is a slap in the face, as it is the European rate, and three times as much as they would have to pay in the States, and it is clear that others are of the same opinion, for sitting at lunch shortly afterwards, a commando hands Alan back the money, indicating they should ask no questions. The crew are very much impressed by this show of support.

The day continues on a high note, when the next weather report indicates that it will be possible to leave tomorrow.

SIXTEEN : LEG FOUR

Greenland to Iceland

Day 12 : Thursday, July 3

"Experienced sailors here don't move inside the ice field when it's like this." (Chief Officer Borg Richs of the Greenland ice patrol station)

At 0800, Alan is summoned to meet the Admiral. Jan and Alan go down to his office. They find him a very amiable man, speaking perfect English, and they chat about Joshua Slocum, Francis Chichester and Alec Rose, and he tells them he is taking up a station at Bracknell in England at the end of the summer, and it would be nice to keep in touch, and would they call in at the end office, on their way out?

The man in the end office hands Jan a piece of paper, which he glances at, hands to Alan and comments that 1100 kroner is reasonable. Alan suggests he looks again at the decimal point; it is a bill for 11,125 kroner (£998), of which 3,600 (£323) is for 3 nights' accommodation, and 7,525 (£675) is for the ship. And the man wants cash. Alan looks at Jan, and they feel as if they have been mugged. They scrape together all the cash they have between them, and it is enough, and Alan makes a mental note to ask the Admiral — some other time — what would have happened if they had been unable to pay there and then. Part of Alan says it is not so bad when they were at one time considering they might lose the boat if they were rescued by helicopter, but on the other hand it is ironic to think that if they had called 'Mayday', there would have been no charge.

Alan has not asked the Danes to sign their arrival and departure certificates, fearing — when they arrived — that if it were highlighted as a timed event, there might be less cooperation, but he has taken the step of faxing James on arrival, and the Danes have agreed to fax James again when *Spirit of Portsmouth* leaves. So the challenge, while somewhat delayed, is still on. Now they must turn their minds forward. To Iceland.

While the latest ice and weather reports are good, the crew are under no illusions about the accuracy of weather forecasting. Wherever they have left, it has been with a perfect forecast and, since it has usually borne little resemblance to reality, they have little faith in them. Yes, they do fly over and actually count the icebergs, but once they have gone the situation can change and no one will know until the next fly-over. However detailed the ice maps are, they can only ever be of limited value in this respect. Rather than be tied down by reams of reports, the crew have learned to prepare for the worst scenario, preferring to use the weather forecasts for comfort more than anything else. Alan is concerned that anyone (daft enough, he says) wanting to follow in their footsteps should take careful note of this.

There is even an argument, sometimes, for not going when the weather is good, but when it is bad, on the assumption that it cannot get any worse. That is something that could apply to any boat trip. Unfortunately, not being experienced in the North Atlantic, it helps to know what 'the worst' can be like; in the open ocean, it is possible to see bad weather coming a long way off, giving some opportunity to manoeuvre round it, but it is the ice which has caused all the major problems, and it is only in the ice that the need for an accurate long-range forecast becomes paramount. A paradox.

In the circumstances, the crew's advice to anyone who does want to follow in the wake of *Spirit of Portsmouth* is leave it later in the year and take three months to do it. It might have been better later, Alan reflects, but one of the things the crew have always prided themselves on is announcing, up to a year before, the dates they are going to start and finish; thus it is a challenge. Someone like Richard Branson who just wants to set a record will wait for the weather to give them the best window. That is not the sort of challenge Alan Priddy wants, because he likes to challenge the elements — whatever the decided window brings. They are two different sorts of challenges.

If someone else <u>was</u> doing this run, the sensible option would be not to do such massive open sea legs. As soon as you increase the distance across open sea, you open up more weather variations. With hindsight (a wonderful thing), shorter hops from point to point across to the east side of Greenland might have stood more chance of success, because fuel would not have been so critical and weather forecasts at shorter range would probably be more accurate.

Part of the problem, too, with long legs between stops, is that small variations in running efficiency become magnified. If for a long leg the boat has to be so full of fuel that it runs inefficiently, then there comes a point at which you gain very little from each extra litre you pack in.

These and many other variations on the same theme are running through the crew's minds as they set off at 0910 with a perfect weather forecast (of course), and the heaviest load so far, but still pulling 30 knots, down the fjord — and to what?

It was perhaps with tongue in cheek that the admiral had told them, an hour before, to "Keep the ice on your left until Cape Farewell, and you'll be OK." There is some ice in the fjord. The crew are in good spirits. It is very cold. Navigation is difficult because of the large-scale charts, and they weave carefully in and out of the rocks, coming eventually to the open sea. They are delighted. There is hardly any ice.

It is rough, though, but they say to each other, we can put up with this. They decide they will go south for 30 miles before turning east, clearing any likelihood of coastal ice. Jan is soon asleep, and Steve notes in the log that it is still very cold. By 1300 they are well clear and, although they still have many miles to go before they pass their original destination, Nanortalik, and then another 60 to Cape Farewell, things are not looking too bad.

No sooner is that thought making them smile despite the bitter air than a bitter realisation comes to them. Suddenly they can see ice on their right hand side. It cannot be, but the further they go, the denser it becomes. They have driven into a dead end, where the ice has hooked, down, round and back up.

There is no alternative but to follow the Admiral's instruction and, still keeping the ice on their left, they are travelling back the way they have come. Fortunately, they have only gone 20 miles into the dead end, but that means 20 miles out again, and they follow it round until at last they are back on their proper course.

About two hours later the same happens again. This time it is heavier ice on their right. Steve wants to find a gap so they do not have to go back again. It could be 70 miles back to open water — as much as crossing the English Channel. They are still discussing it when they spot what looks like a lead to the south east. The decision to try is taken unhesitatingly, and they squeeze through the gap with inches to spare as the ice pack closes grindingly behind them.

From then on, it is more of the same, backwards and forwards though lead after lead, and it is several more hours before they are off Cape Farewell. They have logged 400 miles to travel 180 miles of the journey to Iceland. Alan knows, even at this stage, that even if conditions to Iceland are perfect, fuel is going to be tight. And there is no option but to go on. They cannot go back through the ice, because it is worsening. If they go back, there is nowhere to go.

Alan drives until 2100. He has been driving for 12 hours, and Jan takes over driving with Vic on watch. It has been difficult to get him up from his bunk. He is still suffering from exhaustion and cold, renewed now they are back at sea.

As they round Cape Farewell, there is more ice. More has evidently broken out — it has not been forecast.

At that point something in Alan's head switches off and he is asleep.

Day 13 : Friday, July 4

Steve and Alan need the sleep. They are both nearing exhaustion. Driving a RIB for 12 hours is not like driving a car for a similar time, where the contact with the surface is predictable and there are periods when you can relax. On the RIB, with ice about, and not always visible because of the waves, you have to watch every inch of the way. Small lumps of ice hitting the boat sound dreadful enough, but hitting a bigger one could be catastrophic.

It is 24 hours after leaving Arsuk before they are free of the ice, and they know they are free because the smell has gone and the temperature has risen significantly. And there are no more seals — they had seen many seals on the ice, but fortunately no polar bears. They are all thankful to be clear of the ice — they had hated it, and the smell of it; the smell of the sea, the open sea, gives them new hope.

Alan says much later that he never, ever wants to go back to the Arctic. Or the Antarctic. When he is reminded that he has not been to the Antarctic, he is categorical — he does not want to go there.

Although the seals have gone, and they will miss them, the birds are still plentiful. And a nuisance. They can stop the boat for a rest 400 miles offshore, and within a minute, there are a crowd of birds around the boat. They are mainly large gulls, but sometimes they will find themselves amongst a huge raft of puffins.

At 0745 they are hit by a fierce storm, with force 8 winds and huge, 30 to 40 foot waves crashing down on the boat. The only good thing about it is that it is driving them towards Iceland.

Vic is in a bad way and has been asleep for 12 hours. The gale blows all day, and they lie-to, waiting for a respite. There is none. They can only plod on, hour after hour, driving up the waves, cutting the engine at the top and letting the wave push them a little nearer to their destination, using the minimum of fuel. It is difficult to understand what time it is, what day it is. Jan films some of the time, and shares the driving with Alan. Steve watches. Vic sleeps. The wind blows. The sea is empty save for the *Spirit of Portsmouth* getting nearer, mile by mile, to Iceland. No one talks about fuel. No one talks any more. Now it is just a question of getting as far as they can, as near to civilisation as they can.

The day wears on, and the seas are still big. The North Atlantic is just doing what is has always done, being inhospitable, wearing down its intruders with the steady pressure that needs every ounce of a sailor's strength to counteract it, to stay awake, to stay alive.

Day 14 : Saturday, July 5

North Atlantic

More of the same. The wind is starting to drop, but the seas are still big. They have, during the night, been blown 50 miles closer to Iceland, but still have 100 to go. There is enough fuel for about 50 miles. Out of the grey, there is a ship. They approach it, but are not acknowledged, and they are reminded of the vessel which cooked their radar off Nova Scotia. But on closing with it, with the intention of asking for fuel, they soon see the difference. The boat is fishing, and it has Russian markings, so it is obviously fishing illegally. They are soon alongside, shouting and banging on the rusty hull, but there is no response and no sign of the crew. They do not answer the radio. They would have fuel to run their generators, but Alan can hardly board her and demand it. Besides, he could even be shot. They drive away, disappointed, but hopeful of a more helpful encounter.

Vic is unconscious, going in and out of a comatose state. When he is awake, he says he has been asleep, but Jan is sure he has been unconscious with his exhaustion and hypothermia. Through late afternoon and early evening, the wind rises again, to an estimated gale force 8 or more. It means that they will make no headway in the 40 to 50 foot waves which are building up, and will use more fuel driving up and down the waves than they will use to move forward. They are running down the backs of some of the waves in an effort to surf, but the bow simply dives straight into the next, and fills with freezing water. Even on some occasions when he is completely submerged, Vic does not wake up, and the others are alarmed, and are forced to heave-to again.

The wind is too strong to sail, even though it is behind them, but it is strong enough to force them to drift in the right direction. Mother Nature is being kind, at last, and they are drifting towards Iceland at 5 knots — with enough power to keep the boat headed towards their destination. They drift for 12 hours. It is a miserable existence. Alan drifts in and out of sleep, remembering waking at one point and looking up to see a seagull attacking the little blue knob on the end of the aerial, thinking it is edible. The next minute, he has drifted off again, only to find that seconds later he and Jan are again under water, gasping for breath.

Eventually the wind is dying down, but the seas are still massive, and there are more hours to endure being lifted 40 feet, weightless for an instant, then dropped with a crash. Out in the deep ocean, the steepness of the waves varies considerably, making prediction impossible, and rest difficult. The crew do not like the bad weather — they knew that it was possible, but they didn't come for this.

It is 2050. Crunch time. Reykjavik is just 35 miles away, and the prevailing wind and tide is turning them southwards, away from safety. They are down to their last reserves of fuel. They are not going to get any nearer. Despite sailing into the largest fishing fleet in the world, they have not seen another vessel since the Russian. Time for a chat.

There are few options. Apart from the fuel shortage, Vic is in a very unhappy state, and has been biting his tongue. Jan confirms what they all know — he needs respite from the cold and the battering. They still cannot sail — it is too rough and the wind would blow them the wrong way. There is no one nearby to make contact with by radio — they have been trying — someone who may have fuel. So when all the options are considered, there is only one left. Press the button. But the same dilemma is presented to them as the one they faced in the ice off Arsuk — what help will be sent? Probably a rescue helicopter which would take them to Iceland, and the boat would slowly drift to destruction on some rocky coastline. It would have to be.

The EPIRB system is simple. You just press the button and your position is automatically put out as a distress call via the maritime satellite Cospas-sarsat. *Spirit of Portsmouth*'s signal is actually picked up by Falmouth, but because the equipment is new and the crew have not had chance to personalise it, they are logged as an unidentified vessel in trouble. While the crew wait anxiously in an empty sea, with just manoeuvring fuel left in the main tank, Falmouth is calling Reykjavik by land line, and Reykjavik is calling fishing boats in the area. Little more than two hours later, they are called by an Icelandic fishing boat which has been steaming towards their position. Vic, who has come to, spots them first. Alan sets off a signal flare, and the ship reaches them at 2315.

With a heaving sea between them, there is a short discussion between Alan and the captain of the fishing vessel, *Otto N Thorlaksson*, which has broken off fishing to come to their aid. The captain asks what the crew want to do — come aboard or refuel? Refuelling seems the sensible option, but all they can think of is sleep. There is also the general feeling that it is too rough to refuel with a 300 ton boat rolling alarmingly beside them, and so they break out the lifting gear. It is not easy to connect it up with the violet and different motions of the two boats, and Vic has to be freed when his leg is caught round the cable, and Steve traps his hand, but once connected, within 2 minutes *Spirit of Portsmouth* is on board the *Otto*, and they are making their way below.

Vic is the first priority. He is incoherent and irrational, classic symptoms of severe exhaustion. The others learn from the captain that their message was picked up by the fishing boat before they had started fishing, which was fortunate, because they had been able to come directly. The captain is kindness itself. There is immediate food and coffee placed before them in his quarters. He says he can take them to Reykjavik immediately, but he would like to continue fishing. The crew agree they would benefit from some immediate sleep. They are fed, mattresses are put down on the floor of the cabins and Vic is given the spare bunk. The others have a shower and turn in, too, soon oblivious of the industry going on around them.

Day 15 : Sunday, July 6

North Atlantic

While the *Otto* fishes on through the night, travelling south, the crew of *Spirit of Portsmouth* sleep. Alan, Jan and Steve rise at about 0800, leaving Vic to sleep until lunch time. Jan is concerned, but does not elect to give him medication, because rest is curative and, so far from hospital help, there is no point in risking any reaction to drugs. Vic's muscular structure — the set of his shoulders, ability to walk, even his facial expression — is affected. Jan believes he cannot go on for another leg — if there are problems or delays during the leg to Ireland, he could become critical. The others reluctantly accept Jan's advice.

While they are on the *Otto*, they are fascinated to watch an efficient fishing vessel at work. Within a few hours, there are 220 tons of fish aboard the vessel, which is about the size of a cross-Channel ferry. It is a tough life for the crew, and smelly, but lucrative — the crew can earn £6000 in a month at sea, and the skipper £10000. There are other ships out there in the fleet, and Alan wonders why they had not seen any of them while they were drifting towards Iceland the day before.

On the bridge of the *Otto*, Alan chats easily to the captain: "When we cleared Cape Farewell we knew we didn't have enough fuel to get to Iceland, but we also knew we were sailing into the largest fishing fleet in the world. No problem, we thought. There has to be hundreds of fishing boats out there…"

The skipper's answer is a surprise: "Wrong. When the weather's bad, they don't go out. The weather was bad. They stayed in port." And he adds, with a mischievous Icelandic grin: "Like any sensible sailor would do." Then he looks puzzled. "If you are short of fuel, why didn't you go to the *Arctic Princess*?"

There is a heavy irony in what he says next. The *Arctic Princess* is funded by the fuel companies, and is permanently at sea 200 miles off

Iceland. It is crushingly simple. You telephone any oil company and ask where the ship will be and they give you her position. Alan is speechless, and the captain continues: "There must have been someone you spoke to before who would have known that?' Alan shakes his head. "Oh, well."

They contact the Icelandic Coastguard, principally to thank them, and are informed that, even if they had not set off the EPIRB, in one more hour they would have launched a search and rescue helicopter anyway, because concern was growing as to their safety, so the crew have another reason to thank the captain of the *Otto*. Alan is able to call friends in Iceland and get messages passed home. A little later, Liz is on the telephone directly to the boat — the wonders of modern technology — to speak to Alan in person. They have been concerned at the length of time taken for the crossing. Alan tells her: "I'm never going to leave home again. I've seen enough ice to last me a lifetime." And Steven Redgrave said he would never do another Olympics, and if he did, someone had permission to shoot him. There are some promises which are not meant to be kept. And Liz knows it, even if Alan doesn't. She has already told The News, in Portsmouth: "...I know Alan would be terribly miserable if he couldn't go and do these things. Last time I spoke to him he said he was staying put for a while. I suppose that might last a week or so before he starts thinking about something else — quite what I don't know. I just hope he stays home for a while and gets my decorating done."

By 1500, the *Otto* is hove-to off Reykjavik, and the RIB is being lowered back into the water. At this point Alan is aware that they may have to sacrifice the Guinness Book of Records attempt, because they have accepted outside assistance. But they are not principally concerned about that — the aim was to get from one side of the Atlantic to the other, and 35 miles short is not so bad, considering what they have been through. They will accept it as part of the trip. Steve reminds them that they have done the extra 120 miles north in Greenland anyway, and they all feel much better, especially as they drive with their last dregs of fuel into Reykjavik Harbour, to be greeted by the press, Icelandic TV and their friends.

As they get him off the boat, Vic is already telling Alan he is not going on. Alan can only agree. Over and above his physical problems, Vic's whole mental outlook has changed; his sense of humour and fun is completely gone — another indication of his level of exhaustion.

Iceland is a great place, the crew love it. The food is excellent and, apart from the price of beer at £5 a pint, not as expensive as critics say. They go to the Hard Rock Café, and wish their stay could be longer, but home — and a tightening schedule — calls.

```
Fax: Urgent
To The Hard Rock Café, Reykjavik

For the attention of Bogi Baldersson and the illegal
immigrants from Greenland

Allan, Jan, Steve and Vick

Congratulations on an amazing effort, we have all been
thinking about you (and the money you still owe me).  Our
admiration is not just for your physical achievement but
the suffering endured in sharing a confined space with
Falkowski for more than 60 hours!  Good luck for the rest
of the trip, it's all downhill now.  See you next Saturday
and don't be late!

Tim, Allan, Reg, Mandi and all at the world's finest RIB
building establishment...

RIBTEC
```

There is time to reflect on the achievement so far. They have
travelled from Greenland to Iceland — 982 nautical miles — in 60 hours,
and used 1200 litres of fuel, no mean accomplishment in an open boat.
But, despite the congratulations, it is not over yet. Iceland sits firmly
astride the mid-Atlantic ridge which gives rise to the constant volcanic
activity on and around the island, and so Iceland can be said to be in mid-
Atlantic. There is more to come.

SEVENTEEN : LEG FIVE

Iceland to England

Iceland has been under the rule of one Scandinavian country or another since its first occupation by Norse settlers in 874, according to the 8th Edition of Hutchinson's Encyclopedia. It did not become completely independent until 1944, although it has had its own parliament almost from the beginning. Despite the benefit of the Gulf Stream, Iceland is in nature as it is in name, with much of the country covered by glaciers. But it is a country of extremes, because there are active volcanoes, too, and new islands are being created continuously offshore, Surtsey being the latest in 1963. Being almost totally reliant on fish (one cause of the Cod War in 1976) and latterly tourism for its income, most other goods have to be imported. Iceland has no trees, but power is nevertheless in abundant supply, most being provided by geothermal energy.

The Icelandic language is the oldest Scandinavian language, hardly changed since the 12th century, and the one in which some of the finest sagas were written.

Anyone wishing to find out more about Iceland may find it useful to contact The Icelandic Broadcasting Corporation, Lynghálsi 5, PO Box 10110, IS 130 Reykjavik. For holidays, the brochure issued by Regent Holidays (UK) Limited, 31A High Street, Shanklin IoW PO37 6JW (Telephone 01983-864225, fax -864197) is very informative.

The crew of *Spirit of Portsmouth* are shown to the Guest House, Gisting Og Svefnpokaplass, Tryggvagata 14, 101, in Reykjavik, where Anna Sigurdardóttir welcomes them warmly. It is a pleasure to sleep in a bed, devoid of any movement.

Day 16 : Monday, July 7

They have made arrangements for refuelling, and in the morning, they are asked to go to the other side of the harbour, where Steve and Alan oversee the loading of another 1300 litres of diesel. They know it is going to be a long run.

The weather forecast for Iceland is good (of course), but it is not possible to get an accurate (or even inaccurate) forecast for the considerable amount of ocean between Iceland and Ireland. The only helpful information given to Steve is that: "It's always horrible out there."

They say goodbye to their friends, and especially grateful to Bogi Baldersson and young John Lindsey, who have looked after them so well.

A thorough check of the boat reveals that no maintenance is needed, so the crew can relax for their short stay. Alan makes arrangements to get Vic home, but he will stay there for a day or two to recover before going home. They are very sorry to be leaving him, and feel they are incomplete as they prepare to leave. He does not say goodbye. Their spirits are lifted as once more the engine is fired up and they wend their way out of Reykjavik Harbour. It is 1625 (1525 BST).

With only three in the boat, there is room for ample provisions, and the mood is of home. Iceland quickly disappears below the horizon and all thoughts are forward.

By 2100, with Jan driving, the weather is comfortably warm, and the sea state moderate. There is a south easterly force 2 to 3 blowing, picking up the head seas. At 2350 they see a rainbow forming, and another forming behind it 10 minutes later. They are reminded of McDonald's. The state of the sea gives the impression that there has been a storm and they are heading away from it. It is a false impression.

Day 17 : Tuesday, July 8

As if by the clock, the sea begins to pick up with the new day, and the winds increase to force 5 or 6 . By 0115, with Alan driving, cautiously in the worsening seas, they are already dropping behind schedule. 150 miles south of Iceland they drive straight into a storm.

It is, in Alan's words, the mother of all storms, and brings with it the biggest seas he has ever seen, with waves of up to 60 feet towering over them, coming at them from the south east, relentlessly and savagely. They are glad they have left Vic behind, and wouldn't wish this on anyone, friend or worst enemy. They discuss turning and running before it back to Iceland, but decide that would actually be more dangerous, so they heave-to, reluctantly, to sit it out, the engine off to save fuel.

It is becoming a question of survival. The sea is terrifying, especially for anyone trying to rest. Steve is lying in the bottom of the boat, and hears what he is convinced is a jet engine coming towards him; it stops suddenly, and the boat violently shudders as the wave hits; a split second later, tons of cold water crash into the boat. He holds his breath, willing the pumps to come on; they do, and he floats back down to the deck. It is miserable. And it goes on and on, hour after hour.

The time and space between each of the big waves is unpredictable; while all the seas are big, there might be a predictable spell for 10 minutes, or even an hour, and then they hear the next one; part of them expects the boat to turn over, or to fall apart — everything goes through their minds. They do not actually think they are going to die, but sometimes it takes a special effort <u>not</u> to think it.

Alan starts the engine once each hour to charge the batteries which power the pumps running. Most of the time the boat is full of water to the tops of the tubes. After ten hours they discuss their options. There are none. No storm lasts for ever. But this one seems to.

By the time the wind stops blowing, they have stood it for 18 hours. They know people at home will already be worrying — it should only be a 36 hour crossing, but after 24 hours at sea, they have covered only 79 miles. They try not to think of the satellite communication system they were hoping to take, which would have enabled them to contact England and say they are safe.

Although the wind has stopped, the seas are still mountainous. As conditions improve slowly, they are able to make about 15 knots, but it is excruciatingly hard work. By 2000, the engine is throwing out black smoke because the air filter is blocked with salt, so they quickly replace it. Forward progress is easier now, but the head seas are still big, and it is cold. They estimate they are probably making only 11 or 12 knots over the ground, and once again the question of fuel arises.

At 2350 both GPSs cease working. Alan wriggles below deck and discovers the wiring, attacked by salt water for so many hours, is corroding. In the confined space, he first has to manhandle two full flexible fuel tanks out of the way to jury-rig the wiring. He gets out just in time; another minute and he will have been violently ill.

Day 18 : Wednesday, July 9

By 0400 a thick fog has formed, and with it a calmer sea. Jan and Alan are taking it in turns to drive. They are all very tired, and concerned for people at home, for they are now late, and the radio, with which they could have relayed a message through any shipping they might encounter (they have not done so yet) has taken in so much sea water they are not sure if it is working or not. One of their Irish friends, Garth Henry, is expecting to meet them in his RIB off St Kilda in the Outer Hebrides and, while they know he will wait and wait, they know he will not wait indefinitely. But they can only plod on, getting a little nearer each hour.

By midday they have a serious leak in the starboard flexi-tank, and the loss is not only running them low, it is making the deck treacherously slippery. The stench is awful. It is in their hair, their clothes and on all the equipment. It seems they will never get there.

Day 19 : Thursday, July 10

The weather is becoming much calmer, but tiredness is overtaking them, and at 0230 they shut the boat down and sleep. Waking about an hour later, they hear a call for them on the radio but their equipment will not respond. The crew hope upon hope that no one has pressed the alarm button and a full-scale search is under way for them, even though they are days overdue. But that is exactly what has happened, though not in the way they would have expected.

They are supposed to have attended, with the Mayor, a civic reception in Bangor, and of course have not turned up. The person who is organising the event has been telephoning the coastguard for news, and eventually the coastguard have taken this to mean the travellers are missing. That, however, did not trigger the message heard on the boat which they could not respond to. It was a contributory factor.

Knowing there is a call out for them, the crew decide to head for the nearest point of land, St Kilda, to get a message out by land line. At 0430 they encounter a fishing boat, *Penelope*, who has been lobster potting and is hove-to for the night. They are not impressed when three bedraggled, smelly and piratical-looking sailors bang on the hull. Assured they can get fuel at Barra, the crew of *Spirit of Portsmouth* head for that island at maximum possible speed.

The next unfortunate factor in the chain of misfortunes since leaving Iceland is not going to the naval base, who have a message for them and are looking out for them. At 0600 they are within two miles of Barra, looking for the way in, measuring the height of the islands, when the radio bursts into life. *"Spirit of Portsmouth, Rescue One One, anybody there?"* Alan, Steve and Jan look at each other, all thinking: Oh, no. Full air and sea search. Nimrod. Lifeboats. Oh, no. Alan grabs the radio, praying for it to work: "Rescue One One, *Spirit of Portsmouth*, what can I do for you?" *"Rescue One One. Are you all right?"* "We're fine. Caught in a bad storm." *"Wait one."* Moments later, they relay a message from the coastguard through the plane: *"We'll be with you shortly"*

No sooner have the words died away than across the top of their heads screams the Nimrod, adding aviation fuel to the diesel-soaked boat. Alan looks at Jan, who is at his comfortingly tactful best: "It's 200 grand to launch that plane, Alan." But the crew are puzzled. They are late, but not missing. True, the radio has not been working, but someone has panicked. Someone thinks they are dead. They do not know that all the press bulletins have posted them as missing, driven family members to despair and hyped up the media. Alan shrugs, and answers: "Rescue One One, we are proceeding to Barra for fuel. We do not need assistance."

Famous last words. They are back to the Admiralty chart which clearly shows a passage between two islands. The passage is not there. There is no sea, just land. They circle round, aware that the last of the fuel is rapidly burning away, and eventually decide to go the long way round, down to the next island and through the gap and come up the back side of Barra. Alan warns Jan, who is driving, to go carefully in case of perches which are unmarked on the large scale Admiralty chart, when Steve yells: "Rocks!" They hear the radio again. It is the coastguard, standing on the hilltop, watching them. He explains to them that the gap on the chart has been filled in to make a beach. Evidently no one thought to tell the Admiralty. With the radio still thankfully working he is able to guide them in and they are finally able to step ashore at 0800 to a welcome from what seems like the entire population, swelled by a press contingent.

The press seem to take great delight in telling the crew that the Nimrod has been looking for them for 48 hours, and a Sea King helicopter with heat-seeking equipment for 24 hours, and asking what they think about wasting half a million pounds of taxpayers' money on a stupid adventure? There is more on the mid-morning news. But the people of Barra are superb, and the crew are invited to a hotel to shower, have breakfast and phone home — everyone is crying, and Alan decides they will take it all on the chin and deal with it later. Immediately afterwards, they take on enough fuel to get to Ireland, and leave at 1230. Despite a flat sea and sunshine, they know getting to Portsmouth by Saturday is going to be tight. Alan issues a press release to say they have not been in trouble, just exercising good seamanship in appalling conditions.

At Bangor, they leap ashore at 2020. They have been running for 76 hours since Iceland without sleep. They are greeted by many friends and well-wishers in Bangor, refuel, carry out minimal essential maintenance, and wolf down a meal at the local Chinese restaurant. It is not the best meal they have had on the trip, but it is the quickest.

Fax from Brian Pilcher   To Alan Priddy, c/o Bangor Marina
Welcome back to British soil. Congratulations to you and
the crew — you have conquered the Atlantic!
For the finish at Portsmouth at 1300 hrs, steer for Spit
Sand Fort, from Cowes. To the north of the fort is a
yellow racing buoy called 'Royal Albert'. Richard Spicer
will be aboard a classic RAF launch to record the finish
with cannon fire. Pass between the buoy and the fort,
west to east. Proceed to the foreshore of Southsea, stay
close inshore to let the crowd see you, and proceed at 5
knots to the harbour entrance and slipway.
Congratulations and best wishes.
PS New caps have been sent to Bangor Marina.

During the meal, the truth comes out. The Nimrod has been scrambled — and the Sea King — to look for an Irish fishing boat which has gone missing, and one of Alan's boating friends with the right connections has said to the searchers: "When you're up there, could you put out a call for *Spirit of Portsmouth*, as they are overdue?" The Nimrod has done just that, having known *Spirit of Portsmouth's* whereabouts already by being in touch with the fishing boat *Penelope*, who have informed them where to look. The coastguard, although alerted to the fact that *Spirit of Portsmouth* is considerably overdue, has not actually instituted a search, though they may have done before long.

Alan is upset at those members of the media who have jumped to the wrong conclusions and upset a great number of people, including the crew's families, in their excitement over a potential tragedy. It somehow echoes Brian Pilcher's words about the media being kept informed in case something "interesting" happens. Alan tells The News: "If there was ever any problem we would have used our satellite beacons. It's good to know that people cared enough to worry but we were never in any danger. The boat is designed to withstand this sort of weather."

Apologising to all their friends for the flying visit, the crew rush back to the boat and are away to sea within four hours of landing in Bangor. So much for celebration. But at least they have new caps.

While the excitement has been going on, Vic Palmer has been recovering from the illness which dogged him through the first four legs of the trip. He tells The News he has seen enough icebergs to last a lifetime, and describes the terror of ice passages only 12 feet wide and ice floes bigger than a warehouse superstore, how food poisoning, mountainous waves and seasickness forced him eventually to retire from the Challenge, and how conditions on the voyage were far worse than either he or Alan had anticipated: "I was exhausted and although we had breaks between each route I wasn't well enough to go on. The ice fields got to me. They would just sit there growling at us as they crashed together or water thundered through ice holes." But although Vic has missed the last leg, he will still be able to share with the rest of the crew some of the worst and best memories of the voyage —including the spectacular blood-red sunsets and the seals, whales and dolphins swimming close to the boat.

Vic is grateful to be reunited with his sons, and he is fit enough to travel to meet the crew at Weymouth and rejoin the boat for the final leg to Portsmouth.

Day 20 : Friday, July 11

Leaving Bangor at 0030, they realise it is the first time they have seen darkness for over 10 days. It is strange. As they head out of Belfast Lough, they are praying the weather will be kind in the Irish Sea, because they are running out of time. At that point they decide, come hell or high water, they will stop for fuel anywhere and keep going if necessary, but they will be in Portsmouth for 1300 tomorrow.

Crossing Dublin Bay, the weather deteriorates, and with it the crew's morale. They know they need to maintain 20 knots, and they are down to 4. It is soul-destroying, but they have to battle through. Steve and Alan take an hour's sleep while Jan drives, picking his way carefully through the shipping and the worst of the weather. As the day dawns, the sea becomes flat calm, answering their prayers, and the early morning mist soon clears. Alan takes over, almost nodding off at the wheel at times, while Jan and Steve sleep. Through the day their spirits rise, and the most welcome sight they will ever see is the Seven Sisters Lightship off Penzance. It is still only early afternoon. Alan allows himself to think: nearly home.

Jan and Alan can only drive hour and hour about, they are so tired, and Steve takes a spell, too, while they sleep. He is dead tired, too, and is seeing trees and bushes in front of the boat.

They try to use the mobile phone, but the battery is flat, as they always are. They shrug it off and press on. Alan sets courses for Jan for the Lizard, Eddystone Lighthouse, Start Point and Portland Bill and drifts off to sleep until the Lizard. It is flat all the way. It is as if the sea has done it's worst and has given up trying to drown these determined sailors. At Start Point, Alan radios Brixham Coastguard to ask if they will relay a message to Weymouth — thinking: We're back in civilisation, and we can do these things. Brixham recognise them and relay the message that everyone is waiting for them. The sea is flat at Portland, too, a very rare occurrence.

Half way across Lyme Bay a RIB appears. It is Richard Reddyhoff from Weymouth. He has received the message from Brixham.

There is one last problem to sort out. The medication to constipate the crew has run out in Northern Ireland and there is a new urgency to get to Weymouth. With the press and the world waiting at Weymouth, it might be tricky.

The reception in Weymouth is marvellous, but the three crewmen have to confess to enthusiastic photographers that they cannot stop. They need the toilets. Right now. After that, they rejoin the press and well-wishers, and are delighted to have a rejuvenated Vic back with them.

Members of the Royal Dorset Yacht Club are waiting for them, taking them by car for a lovely meal and presenting them with a superb silver plaque. In a quiet moment, they note that they have logged 1000 miles in the last 101 hours, without going to bed. They have pushed themselves to the limit.

But they still manage to party until about 1 o'clock in the morning in the RDYC and in the hotel afterwards, and it is 106 hours before they finally see a bed. They turn in and pass out.

Day 21 : Saturday, July 12

The Last Lap

Steve and Alan have booked an early morning call to get the boat ready. There is a knock on the door at 0630. Alan takes two paces and his legs collapse under him. After an hour, he makes it wearily down to the boat, where they get out the detergent and set to cleaning up the spilt diesel. It looks presentable enough by breakfast time, and they return to meet the rest of the severely hung over crew and friends. They meet Jonathan Smith of The News; he is to accompany them home.

Leaving Weymouth at 1000, it is a wonderful run up the Dorset coast, Alan pointing out to Jonathan the rock climbs, and Lulworth and Durdle Dor. It seems forever since they last passed this way.

But the most emotional part of the trip is seeing all their friends at the Needles — 40 RIBs from all over England, friends and family, including James, Wayne, Leah and Kelly and, as the flotilla progresses, more and more boats accumulating. It is a spectacular run down through the Solent, scores of sailing boats wondering what is happening as the powerboats turn the water white from Hurst Castle to Southsea. The crowds on shore begin at the Sea Life Centre and stretch right the way along; the round tower is full to overflowing. Coming in from the sea, leading the pack, the crew of *Spirit of Portsmouth* can see just a mass of coloured dots and white water. Even the defence police are surprised to see so many boats supporting the homecoming. Having tried and failed to get the TV and press to share the cost of a helicopter, Alan smiles to himself as he imagines them regretting that decision.

They cross the line at 1258, just two minutes ahead of schedule, and drive proudly round to Camber Dock.

To get the boat on the trailer is a military exercise. The power trim has broken and they cannot lift the gearbox up, so everyone has to do things in order, but it is perfection. As he winches the boat on to the waiting truck, Tim Wilks of Ribtec has a chance to look quickly round the hull. He cannot believe it is undamaged.

The jubilant crew, still in the boat, offer their frostbitten hands to a sea of well-wishers on the two hundred yard final journey to the Bridge Tavern. Willing hands help them down and on to the rostrum, where the Mayor of Portsmouth, Tony Golds, greets them. Jerry Wilson has done a superb job of organising the homecoming. There is champagne, a magnificent glass trophy, and speeches, but the crew are too overwhelmed with the welcome to take much of it in. They will have to watch it later.

There are some nuns in the crowd; some astute members of the public notice they are wearing make-up. They call Alan over and one says they are from some convent or other, and as he has been at sea for such a long time, would he like a good seeing-to? Alan says the only thing a man in this situation can say: "What?" She shows him what. But he is too tired to care. Nevertheless, the celebrations at the Bridge Tavern, and at the barbecue outside, keep the crew going until after midnight, when the last reserves of energy drain from their bodies. Now there are just memories. Perhaps the most abiding one is an appreciative and respectful crowd listening to Alan, saying:

"If anyone says to you 'It's cold out there', you don't know what cold is. If someone says 'That's rough', they don't know what rough is. If anyone says 'That's scary', they don't know what scared is." He means it. But you have to be there, really.

EIGHTEEN : FOLLOW THAT

The next morning, Sunday, Alan gets up about 11 am, and goes down to the boat and takes everything off, muttering about needing a holiday. His feet are sore and it will be a few days before he can walk properly. He takes a last look at the boat before he leaves to spend a few hours at home before going back to work tomorrow. It will all take time to sink in. The 1000 photographs and 9 hours of video will help.

On her trip of a lifetime, *Still Never Enough*, alias *Spirit of Portsmouth*, has spent some 270 hours at sea and covered 5979 nautical miles at an average speed of nearly 18 knots. She is still in one piece, as a closer inspection of boat, engine and all of the equipment, including clothing, shows.

The same cannot be said for her crew. They did not expect it to be easy, but it has been harder than they thought it would be. The cold and bad weather have taken their toll, causing exhaustion, mild hypothermia and frostbite. But all that is recoverable, and it will not be long before they are planning their next adventure.

There are some amusing points to recall. Steve is happy with the waterproof notebooks in which he kept a log — unfortunately he did not try writing at 30 knots before starting out. Some of it is difficult to decipher, to say the least. Steve is also delighted with the Musto suit; there is a small patch of wear on the arm where it has been in constant contact with the guard rail. Not bad for 6000 miles, he says.

Jan later confirms the frostbite will heal and there is no permanent damage done. Vic is fully recovered and his old jovial self. Even he is looking forward to the next one. The News notes with pride that the crew have not been asked for their passports once on the whole trip.

Alan is now working hard for a good stand at the London Boat Show in January 1998 in conjunction with their loyal and generous sponsors, and also for some long-overdue TV coverage.

It is an interesting fact that, although Yamaha have not looked at the engine, as they trust Alan implicitly to give them feedback, they are very happy. No one else has run that engine for that length of time before, and certainly not under such extreme conditions. You can run an engine for 1000 hours on a test bench, but it's not the same. They have pledged their support for the next 2 years. Vic and Alan have stripped the engine down since, and found nothing amiss.

For a trip such as this, Alan advises, more attention should be paid to sleeping arrangements, since they did not catch up the entire journey, and took about six weeks afterwards to do so. It was partly to do with the lack of darkness, but it has an enormous effect on efficiency.

And finally, the next trip. I ask him (a month later) how he feels about the next trip. Liz gets in first: "He's taking up golf."

Alan is allowed to reply: "I didn't really want to do a trip next year, but there's a good argument for keeping the pot boiling. At the moment, the sponsorship is good. London to Monte Carlo hasn't been attempted for some 20 years. It's 2000 miles. That's a lot, unassisted, and it's never been done in a RIB, so we'll probably do that. It's mercenary, because I want the boat in the Mediterranean next year. It would be nice to go out there say once a month and have the boat waiting. There is a route through France... a friend of mine has just done it. It takes three to four weeks. You're restricted to 5 knots, and there are about 900 locks! It isn't for me.

"We're also considering an American trip, New York to San Francisco, through the Panama Canal. I'm not considering the clipper route round Cape Horn, because I'm not keen on going down towards Antarctica! It's an enormously long route, possibly further than round the world. The Panama route is also easily commutable from Heathrow, and we thought civilisation would be a nice change. Besides, the feedback we got from America tells us that we'd have no trouble getting sponsors out there for such a trip.

"You'd have a job, though, to do anything more dramatic than the North Atlantic, although the North West Passage was discussed. I'm not doing that, although it could be done with a standby helicopter. "

He has been challenged to go from New York to London non-stop in 1999, but fuel would be a problem. "You would need at least one fuel dump somewhere in the middle, so you'd have to meet a ship. It's less challenging than what we've done this year. We might not accept the challenge. Olympic year might not be a bad idea, round Australia, Sydney to Sydney, but there's a severe shortage of pubs on route..."

What about round the Equator? "As I'm going on," says Alan, "I'd much rather go to places that speak English. It's so much more civilised."

To all our friends we have met while
'Beating the Big One'.
It is now Monday morning and some 36 hours since we crossed the finishing line as promised off Southsea seafront. There were times that this mission seemed impossible due to very bad weather or the ice conditions up in the Arctic, but with true determination and perhaps sometimes stupidity we battled on to cross the finishing line as planned. Once again, on behalf of the crew of Still Never Enough, I would like to thank all of you for your help and support (especially the huge number of RIBs that met us off the Needles) in making this trip a true adventure in every aspect... With best regards to you all. Alan Priddy

WELL DONE, YOU MADE IT!!!!
Congratulations from the City of Portsmouth, NH. The City has
tracked your progress carefully and are pleased to learn of
your successful completion of the arduous journey. We hope to
see you in the future.

from Mike, Val, Spencer, Aston, Fraser and "Otis" Verlander
CONGRATULATIONS
Our heartfelt congratulations to you all on the completion of
your epic voyage. Hoping you enjoy your homecoming reception
and receive the credit you all so richly deserve. Once again,
well done and have a great day. Otis sends special regards to
Alan and Vic!! Remember us when you are having a cold one
(beer that is).

from the Marconi Family
YOU MADE IT!!!!
Congratulations from Bea and the entire Marconi family and the
friends you all made during your stay in Portsmouth. We have
all followed your progress and are so pleased and thankful that
you have arrived safe and sound. We are pleased to have been
associated with you all in preparation for your trip. Kind
regards and very best wishes, Bea and your family of friends
from Portsmouth NH

from David Brettell, Henshaw Inflatables
WHAT A FANTASTIC FEAT. CONGRATULATIONS AND WELCOME HOME

Congratulations on the completion of your Atlantic Challenge.
Greetings from North Sydney. We were so glad to receive the
fax that you had arrived in Ireland. Our thoughts and prayers
were with you and your families as word filtered in that you
hadn't arrived. I have some photos of your stay with us that I
will mail to you soon. Hope to hear from you again and maybe
get some footage or pictures of your voyage. Take care and all
the best.
Natalie Marsh and Harry King.

From Don Gosden, Operations Director   16 July 1997
Congratulations on a job well done.
From your report the team do not appear to have had an easy
time and on some of the legs the elements seem to have done
their best to frustrate the challenge. I hope our tanks did
their job without problems. Thank you for keeping us informed
of progress — very much appreciated.
Kind regards from all at Air Cushion Ltd

INDEX (Bold numbers are chapters)

Agdlek 102
Air Cushions Ltd 66, 70, 127
Allan & Bath 70
Arsuk 100-1
Baldersson, Bogi 115, 116
Bangor, N Ireland 12, 32, 35, 49, 119-22
Barra 119-20
Battle Harbour 49, 76, 91, **15**
Budd, Tim & Gary **2**
Camarc 63
Cameron, Alastair 63
Cancer Care Society 50, 74
Concept Interiors 70
Couzens, T & Sons 71
Critchley, Martin 15
Devonshire Estates 71
Falkowski, Jan (biographical) **6**
Finnimore, Richard 59
Foley, Eileen 50, 51, 71, 77
Gales 71
Glicksberg, B **2**
Golds, Tony 124
Greenland 103, **15, 16**
Hart, Wes 76, 80
Hempsall, Simon 58
Henry, Garth 32, 71, 118
Henshaw Inflatables 64, 71
Hilsea Engineers 71
Holloway, Paul 82
Iceland **16, 17**
IMS 58-9, 72
Isle of Wight 12, (round) 75
King, Harry 88, 127
Labrador 77, 92, **15**
Lawson, S **2**
Lindsey, John 116
Lloyd, Steve (biographical) **6**
Lyndhurst School 72
McCarthy, Lester 32
McKenna, Shaun 72
McLeod, Dr Louise 87
Marconi, Beatrice 72, 83, 127
Marsh, Natalie 76, 87, 88
Musto 38, 40, 44, 57, 60, 67-9, 125
Nanortalik 100

Nielson, Per 72, 97
North Sydney Rotary 87, 88
O'Neill, Denis 32
Otto N Thorlaksson 112
Paddon, Tom 93
Palmer, Vic (biographical) **6**
Pendleton, Mike 82, 84
Penelope 119
Peters & May 72
Pilcher, Brian 47, 57, 76, 81, 84, 120
Poole, Keith 76, 95-7
Portsmouth, UK 73, 123
Portsmouth, USA 72, **12, 13**
Poulter, Joe 65, 88
Priddy, Alan (biographical) **6**
Priddy, James 53, 59
Priority Stainless 73
Raytheon 82, 84, 98
Reddyhoff, Richard 15, 122
Reykjavik 114
Ribtec Limited 24, 49, 61, 78,
          115, 124
Richs, Borg 107
Rosemead Developments 73
Royal Dorset Yacht Club 54, 123
Royal Mail Social Club 73
Royal Naval Club & Royal Albert
          Yacht Club — see Spicer
Russell, Alan & Reg 62-3
Sigurdardóttir, Anna 116
Smith, Jonathan 73, 83, 123
Southsea Castle Rotary Club 73
Spicer, Richard 60, 120
Sydney, Nova Scotia 86-9
Travel Planners 73
Verlander, Val & Mike 73, 82, 127
Wallaneus 73, 76
Waroux, Jean-Pierre **2, 3**
Wentworth Marina 52, 72, 82
Weymouth 122
White Light 73
Wilks, Tim 61, 124
Wilson, Jerry 58-9, 72, 124
Yamaha 49, 65-6, 75, 88, 125

Greenland: Everyone is amazed the boat is undamaged

Greenland: Powering out of Arsuk fjord, spirits are high again

Iceland: Alan and the skipper of Otto, Sigurdur Steindórsson

North Atlantic: No horizon, but always seagulls

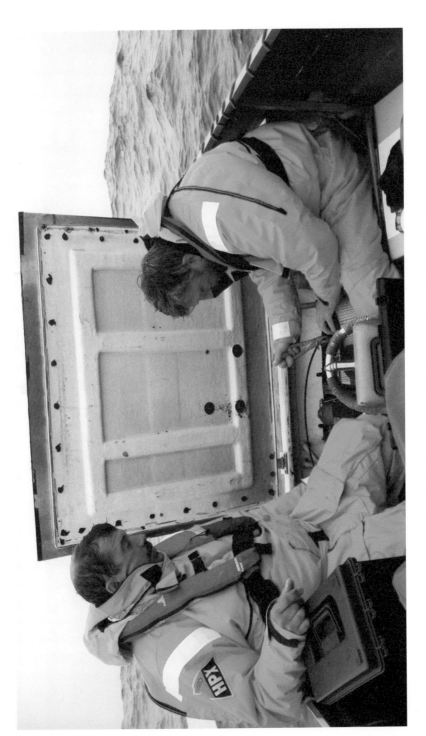

South of Iceland: Changing the air filter in the huge swell

Portsmouth, UK: One last hitch, watched by enthusiastic crowds

Portsmouth, UK: Pupils of Lyndhurst School, North End

News has reached the top…